Caffe2 Quick Start Guide

Modular and scalable deep learning made easy

Ashwin Nanjappa

BIRMINGHAM - MUMBAI

Caffe2 Quick Start Guide

Copyright © 2019 Packt Publishing

Commissioning Editor: Amey Varangaonkar
Acquisition Editor: Siddharth Mandal
Content Development Editor: Mohammed Yusuf Imaratwale
Technical Editor: Rutuja Vaze
Copy Editor: Safis Editing
Project Coordinator: Kinjal Bari
Proofreader: Safis Editing
Indexer: Pratik Shirodkar
Graphics: Jason Monteiro
Production Coordinator: Jyoti Chauhan

First published: May 2019

Production reference: 1310519

Published by Packt Publishing Ltd.
Livery Place
35 Livery Street
Birmingham
B3 2PB, UK.

ISBN 978-1-78913-775-0

www.packtpub.com

`mapt.io`

Mapt is an online digital library that gives you full access to over 5,000 books and videos, as well as industry leading tools to help you plan your personal development and advance your career. For more information, please visit our website.

Why subscribe?

- Spend less time learning and more time coding with practical eBooks and Videos from over 4,000 industry professionals

- Improve your learning with Skill Plans built especially for you

- Get a free eBook or video every month

- Mapt is fully searchable

- Copy and paste, print, and bookmark content

Packt.com

Did you know that Packt offers eBook versions of every book published, with PDF and ePub files available? You can upgrade to the eBook version at `www.packt.com` and as a print book customer, you are entitled to a discount on the eBook copy. Get in touch with us at `customercare@packtpub.com` for more details.

At `www.packt.com`, you can also read a collection of free technical articles, sign up for a range of free newsletters, and receive exclusive discounts and offers on Packt books and eBooks.

Contributors

About the author

Ashwin Nanjappa is a senior architect at NVIDIA, working in the TensorRT team on improving deep learning inference on GPU accelerators. He has a PhD from the National University of Singapore in developing GPU algorithms for the fundamental computational geometry problem of 3D Delaunay triangulation. As a post-doctoral research fellow at the BioInformatics Institute (Singapore), he developed GPU-accelerated machine learning algorithms for pose estimation using depth cameras. As an algorithms research engineer at Visenze (Singapore), he implemented computer vision algorithm pipelines in C++, developed a training framework built upon Caffe in Python, and trained deep learning models for some of the world's most popular online shopping portals.

About the reviewers

Gianni Rosa Gallina is an Italian senior software engineer and architect who has been focused on emerging technologies, AI, and virtual/augmented reality since 2013. Currently, he works in Deltatre's Innovation Lab, prototyping solutions for next-generation sport experiences and business services. Besides that, he has 10+ years of certified experience as consultant on Microsoft and .NET technologies (including technologies such as the Internet of Things, the cloud, and desktop/mobile apps). Since 2011, he has been awarded Microsoft MVP in the Windows Development category. He has been a Pluralsight Author since 2013 and is a speaker at national and international conferences.

Ryan Riley has been in the futures and derivatives industry for almost 20 years. He received bachelor's and master's degrees from DePaul University in applied statistics. Doing his coursework in math meant he had to teach himself how to program, thus forcing him to read more technical books on programming than someone would otherwise. Ryan has worked with numerous AI libraries in various languages and is currently using the Caffe2 C++ library to develop and implement futures and derivatives trading strategies at PNT Financial.

Packt is searching for authors like you

If you're interested in becoming an author for Packt, please visit `authors.packtpub.com` and apply today. We have worked with thousands of developers and tech professionals, just like you, to help them share their insight with the global tech community. You can make a general application, apply for a specific hot topic that we are recruiting an author for, or submit your own idea.

Table of Contents

Preface

Caffe2 is a popular deep learning framework designed with a focus on scalability, high performance, and portability. Written in C++, it has both a C++ API and a Python API. This book is a guide for you to quickly get started with Caffe2. It will cover the topics of installing Caffe2, composing networks using its operators, training models, and deploying models to inference engines, devices at the edge, and the cloud. It will also show you how to work with Caffe2 and other deep learning frameworks using the ONNX interchange format.

Who this book is for

Data scientists and machine learning engineers who wish to create fast and scalable deep learning models in Caffe2 will find this book to be very useful.

What this book covers

Chapter 1, *Introduction and Installation*, introduces Caffe2 and examines how to build and install it.

Chapter 2, *Composing Networks*, teaches you about Caffe2 operators and how to compose them to build a simple computation graph and a neural network to recognize handwritten digits.

Chapter 3, *Training Networks*, gets into how to use Caffe2 to compose a network for training and how to train a network to solve the MNIST problem.

Chapter 4, *Working with Caffe*, explores the relationship between Caffe and Caffe2 and how to work with models trained in Caffe.

Chapter 5, *Working with Other Frameworks*, looks at contemporary deep learning frameworks such as TensorFlow and PyTorch and how we can exchange models from and to Caffe2 and these other frameworks.

Chapter 6, *Deploying Models to Accelerators for Inference*, talks about inference engines and how they are an essential tool for the final deployment of a trained Caffe2 model on accelerators. We focus on two types of popular accelerators: NVIDIA GPUs and Intel CPUs. We look at how to install and use TensorRT for deploying our Caffe2 model on NVIDIA GPUs. We also look at the installation and use of OpenVINO for deploying our Caffe2 model on Intel CPUs and accelerators.

Chapter 7, *Caffe2 at the Edge and in the cloud*, covers two applications of Caffe2 to demonstrate its ability to scale. As an application of Caffe2 with edge devices, we look at how to build Caffe2 on Raspberry Pi single-board computers and how to run Caffe2 applications on them. As an application of Caffe2 with the cloud, we look at the use of Caffe2 in Docker containers.

To get the most out of this book

Some understanding of basic machine learning concepts and prior exposure to programming languages such as C++ and Python will be useful.

Download the example code files

You can download the example code files for this book from your account at www.packt.com. If you purchased this book elsewhere, you can visit www.packt.com/support and register to have the files emailed directly to you.

You can download the code files by following these steps:

1. Log in or register at www.packt.com.
2. Select the **SUPPORT** tab.
3. Click on **Code Downloads & Errata**.
4. Enter the name of the book in the **Search** box and follow the onscreen instructions.

Once the file is downloaded, please make sure that you unzip or extract the folder using the latest version of:

- WinRAR/7-Zip for Windows
- Zipeg/iZip/UnRarX for Mac
- 7-Zip/PeaZip for Linux

The code bundle for the book is also hosted on GitHub at `https://github.com/PacktPublishing/Caffe2-Quick-Start-Guide`. In case there's an update to the code, it will be updated on the existing GitHub repository.

We also have other code bundles from our rich catalog of books and videos available at `https://github.com/PacktPublishing/`. Check them out!

Conventions used

There are a number of text conventions used throughout this book.

`CodeInText`: Indicates code words in text, database table names, folder names, filenames, file extensions, pathnames, dummy URLs, user input, and Twitter handles. Here is an example: "The output values of a `SoftMax` function have nice properties."

A block of code is set as follows:

```
model = model_helper.ModelHelper("MatMul model")
model.net.MatMul(["A", "B"], "C")
```

Any command-line input or output is written as follows:

```
$ sudo apt-get update
```

Bold: Indicates a new term, an important word, or words that you see onscreen. For example, words in menus or dialog boxes appear in the text like this. Here is an example: " For example, for Ubuntu, it gives me the option of downloading a **Customizable Package** or a single large **Full Package**."

Warnings or important notes appear like this.

Tips and tricks appear like this.

Get in touch

Feedback from our readers is always welcome.

General feedback: If you have questions about any aspect of this book, mention the book title in the subject of your message and email us at customercare@packtpub.com.

Errata: Although we have taken every care to ensure the accuracy of our content, mistakes do happen. If you have found a mistake in this book, we would be grateful if you would report this to us. Please visit www.packt.com/submit-errata, selecting your book, clicking on the Errata Submission Form link, and entering the details.

Piracy: If you come across any illegal copies of our works in any form on the Internet, we would be grateful if you would provide us with the location address or website name. Please contact us at copyright@packt.com with a link to the material.

If you are interested in becoming an author: If there is a topic that you have expertise in and you are interested in either writing or contributing to a book, please visit authors.packtpub.com.

Reviews

Please leave a review. Once you have read and used this book, why not leave a review on the site that you purchased it from? Potential readers can then see and use your unbiased opinion to make purchase decisions, we at Packt can understand what you think about our products, and our authors can see your feedback on their book. Thank you!

For more information about Packt, please visit packt.com.

Introduction and Installation

1

Welcome to the Caffe2 Quick Start Guide. This book aims to provide you with a quick introduction to the Caffe2 deep learning framework and how to use it for training and deployment of deep learning models. This book uses code samples to create, train, and run inference on actual deep learning models that solve real problems. In this way, its code can be applied quickly by readers to their own applications.

This chapter provides a brief introduction to Caffe2 and shows you how to build and install it on your computer. In this chapter, we will cover the following topics:

- Introduction to deep learning and Caffe2
- Building and installing Caffe2
- Testing Caffe2 Python API
- Testing Caffe2 C++ API

Introduction to deep learning

Terms such as **artificial intelligence** (**AI**), **machine learning** (**ML**), and **deep learning** (**DL**) are popular right now. This popularity can be attributed to significant improvements that deep learning techniques have brought about in the last few years in enabling computers to see, hear, read, and create. First and foremost, we'll introduce these three fields and how they intersect:

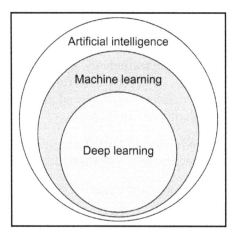

Figure 1.1: Relationship between deep learning, ML, and AI

AI

Artificial intelligence (**AI**) is a general term used to refer to the intelligence of computers, specifically their ability to reason, sense, perceive, and respond. It is used to refer to any non-biological system that has intelligence, and this intelligence is a consequence of a set of rules. It does not matter in AI if those sets of rules were created manually by a human, or if those rules were automatically learned by a computer by analyzing data. Research into AI started in 1956, and it has been through many ups and a couple of downs, called **AI winters**, since then.

ML

Machine learning (ML) is a subset of AI that uses statistics, data, and learning algorithms to teach computers to learn from given data. This data, called **training data**, is specific to the problem being solved, and contains examples of input and the expected output for each input. ML algorithms learn models or representations automatically from training data, and these models can be used to obtain predictions for new input data.

There are many popular types of models in ML, including **artificial neural networks (ANNs)**, Bayesian networks, **support vector machines (SVM)**, and random forests. The ML model that is of interest to us in this book is ANN. The structure of ANNs are inspired by the connections in the brain. These neural network models were initially popular in ML, but later fell out of favor since they required enormous computing power that was not available at that time.

Deep learning

Over the last decade, utilization of the parallel processing capability of **graphics processing units (GPUs)** to solve general computation problems became popular. This type of computation came to be known as **general-purpose computing on GPU (GPGPU)**. GPUs were quite affordable and were easy to use as accelerators by using GPGPU programming models and APIs such as **Compute Unified Device Architecture (CUDA)** and **Open Computing Language (OpenCL)**. Starting in 2012, neural network researchers harnessed GPUs to train neural networks with a large number of layers and started to generate breakthroughs in solving computer vision, speech recognition, and other problems. The use of such deep neural networks with a large number of layers of neurons gave rise to the term **deep learning**. Deep learning algorithms form a subset of ML and use multiple layers of abstraction to learn and parameterize multi-layer neural network models of data.

Introduction to Caffe2

The popularity and success of deep learning has been motivated by the creation of many popular and open source deep learning frameworks that can be used for training and inference of neural networks. **Caffe** was one of the first popular deep learning frameworks. It was created by *Yangqing Jia* at UC Berkeley for his PhD thesis and released to the public at the end of 2013. It was primarily written in C++ and provided a C++ API. Caffe also provided a rudimentary Python API wrapped around the C++ API. The Caffe framework created networks using layers. Users created networks by listing down and describing its layers in a text file commonly referred to as a **prototxt**.

Following the popularity of Caffe, universities, corporations, and individuals created and launched many deep learning frameworks. Some of the popular ones today are Caffe2, TensorFlow, MXNet, and PyTorch. TensorFlow is driven by Google, MXNet has the support of Amazon, and PyTorch was primarily developed by Facebook.

Caffe's creator, Yangqing Jia, moved to Facebook, where he created a follow-up to Caffe called Caffe2. Compared to the other deep learning frameworks, Caffe2 was designed to focus on scalability, high performance, and portability. Written in C++, it has both a C++ API and a Python API.

Caffe2 and PyTorch

Caffe2 and PyTorch are both popular DL frameworks, maintained and driven by Facebook. PyTorch originates from the **Torch** DL framework. It is characterized by a Python API that is easy for designing different network structures and experimenting with training parameters and regimens on them. While PyTorch could be used for inference in production applications on the cloud and in the edge, it is not as efficient when it comes to this.

Caffe2 has a Python API and a C++ API. It is designed for practitioners who tinker with existing network structures and use pre-trained models from PyTorch, Caffe, and other DL frameworks, and ready them for deployment inside applications, local workstations, low-power devices at the edge, mobile devices, and in the cloud.

Having observed the complementary features of PyTorch and Caffe2, Facebook has a plan to merge the two projects. As we will see later, Caffe2 source code is already organized as a subdirectory under the PyTorch Git repository. In the future, expect more intermingling of these two projects, with a final goal of fusing the two together to create a single DL framework that is easy to experiment with and tinker, efficient to train and deploy, and that can scale from the cloud to the edge, from general-purpose processors to special-purpose accelerators.

Hardware requirements

Working with deep learning models, especially the training process, requires a lot of computing power. While you could train a popular neural network on the CPU, it could typically take many hours or days, depending on the complexity of the network. Using GPUs for training is highly recommended since they typically reduce the training time by an order of magnitude or more compared to CPUs. Caffe2 uses CUDA to access the parallel processing capabilities of NVIDIA GPUs. CUDA is an API that enables developers to use the parallel computation capabilities of an NVIDIA GPU, so you will need to use an NVIDIA GPU. You can either install an NVIDIA GPU on your local computer, or use a cloud service provider such as Amazon AWS that provides instances with NVIDIA GPUs. Please take note of the running costs of such cloud instances before you use them for extended periods of training.

Once you have trained a model using Caffe2, you can use CPUs, GPUs, or many other processors for inference. We will explore a few such options in Chapter 6, *Deploying Models to Accelerators for Inference*, and Chapter 7, *Caffe2 at the Edge and in the cloud*, later in the book.

Software requirements

A major portion of deep learning research and development is currently taking place on Linux computers. **Ubuntu** is a distribution of Linux that happens to be very popular for deep learning research and development. We will be using Ubuntu as the operating system of choice in this book. If you are using a different flavor of Linux, you should be able to search online for commands similar to Ubuntu commands for most of the operations described here. If you use Windows or macOS, you will need to replace the Linux commands in this book with equivalent commands. All the code samples should work on Linux, Windows, and macOS with zero or minimal changes.

Building and installing Caffe2

Caffe2 can be built and installed from source code quite easily. Installing Caffe2 from source gives us more flexibility and control over our application setup. The build and install process has four stages:

1. Installing dependencies
2. Installing acceleration libraries

3. Building Caffe2
4. Installing Caffe2

Installing dependencies

We first need to install packages that Caffe2 is dependent on, as well as the tools and libraries required to build it.

1. First, obtain information about the newest versions of Ubuntu packages by querying their online repositories using the `apt-get` tool:

   ```
   $ sudo apt-get update
   ```

2. Next, using the `apt-get` tool, install the libraries that are required to build Caffe2, and that Caffe2 requires for its operation:

   ```
   $ sudo apt-get install -y --no-install-recommends \
         build-essential \
         cmake \
         git \
         libgflags2 \
         libgoogle-glog-dev \
         libgtest-dev \
         libiomp-dev \
         libleveldb-dev \
         liblmdb-dev \
         libopencv-dev \
         libopenmpi-dev \
         libsnappy-dev \
         libprotobuf-dev \
         openmpi-bin \
         openmpi-doc \
         protobuf-compiler \
         python-dev \
         python-pip
   ```

   These packages include tools required to download Caffe2 source code (Git) and to build Caffe2 (`build-essential`, `cmake`, and `python-dev`). The rest are libraries that Caffe2 is dependent on, including Google Flags (`libgflags2`), Google Log (`libgoogle-glog-dev`), Google Test (`libgtest-dev`), LevelDB (`libleveldb-dev`), LMDB (`liblmdb-dev`), OpenCV (`libopencv-dev`), OpenMP (`libiomp-dev`), OpenMPI (`openmpi-bin` and `openmpi-doc`), Protobuf (`libprotobuf-dev` and `protobuf-compiler`), and Snappy (`libsnappy-dev`).

3. Finally, install the Python Pip tool and use it to install other Python libraries such as `NumPy` and `Protobuf` Python APIs that are useful when working with Python:

```
$ sudo apt-get install -y --no-install-recommends python-pip
```

```
$ pip install --user \
      future \
      numpy \
      protobuf
```

Installing acceleration libraries

Using Caffe2 to train DL networks and using them for inference involves a lot of math computation. Using acceleration libraries of math routines and deep learning primitives helps Caffe2 users by speeding up training and inference tasks. Vendors of CPUs and GPUs typically offer such libraries, and Caffe2 has support to use such libraries if they are available on your system.

Intel Math Kernel Library (MKL) is key to faster training and inference on Intel CPUs. This library is free for personal and community use. It can be downloaded by registering here: `https://software.seek.intel.com/performance-libraries`. Installation involves uncompressing the downloaded package and running the `install.sh` installer script as a superuser. The library files are installed by default to the `/opt/intel` directory. The Caffe2 build step, described in the next section, finds and uses the BLAS and LAPACK routines of MKL automatically, if MKL was installed at the default directory.

CUDA and **CUDA Deep Neural Network (cuDNN)** libraries are essential for faster training and inference on NVIDIA GPUs. CUDA is free to download after registering here: `https://developer.nvidia.com/cuda-downloads`. cuDNN can be downloaded from here: `https://developer.nvidia.com/cudnn`. Note that you need to have a modern NVIDIA GPU and an NVIDIA GPU driver already installed. As an alternative to the GPU driver, you could use the driver that is installed along with CUDA. Files of the CUDA and cuDNN libraries are typically installed in the `/usr/local/cuda` directory on Linux. The Caffe2 build step, described in the next section, finds and uses CUDA and cuDNN automatically if installed in the default directory.

Building Caffe2

Using Git, we can clone the Git repository containing Caffe2 source code and all the submodules it requires:

```
$ git clone --recursive https://github.com/pytorch/pytorch.git && cd
pytorch

$ git submodule update --init
```

Notice how the Caffe2 source code now exists in a subdirectory inside the PyTorch source repository. This is because of Facebook's cohabitation plan for these two popular DL frameworks as it endeavors to merge the best features of both frameworks over a period of time.

Caffe2 uses CMake as its build system. CMake enables Caffe2 to be easily built for a wide variety of compilers and operating systems.

To build Caffe2 source code using CMake, we first create a build directory and invoke CMake from within it:

```
$ mkdir build
$ cd build
$ cmake ..
```

CMake checks available compilers, operating systems, libraries, and packages, and figures out which Caffe2 features to enable and compilation options to use. These options can be seen listed in the CMakeLists.txt file present at the root directory. Options are listed in the form of option(USE_FOOBAR "Use Foobar library" OFF). You can enable or disable those options by setting them to ON or OFF in CMakeLists.txt.

These options can also be configured when invoking CMake. For example, if your Intel CPU has support for AVX/AVX2/FMA, and you would wish to use those features to speed up Caffe2 operations, then enable the USE_NATIVE_ARCH option as follows:

```
$ cmake -DUSE_NATIVE_ARCH=ON ..
```

Installing Caffe2

CMake produces a Makefile file at the end. We can build Caffe2 and install it on our system using the following command:

```
$ sudo make install
```

This step involves building a large number of CUDA files, which can be very slow. It is recommended to use the parallel execution feature of `make` to use all the cores of your CPU for a faster build. We can do this by using the following command:

```
$ sudo make -j install
```

Using the `make` install method to build and install makes it difficult to update or uninstall Caffe2 later.
Instead, I prefer to create a Debian package of Caffe2 and install it. That way, I can uninstall or update it conveniently. We can do this using the `checkinstall` tool.

To install `checkinstall`, and to use it to build and install Caffe2, use the following commands:

```
$ sudo apt-get install checkinstall
$ sudo checkinstall --pkgname caffe2
```

This command also produces a Debian `.deb` package file that you can use to install on other computers or share with others. For example, on my computer, this command produced a file named `caffe2_20181207-1_amd64.deb`.

If you need a faster build, use the parallel execution feature of `make` along with `checkinstall`:

```
$ sudo checkinstall --pkgname caffe2 make -j install
```

If you need to uninstall Caffe2 in the future, you can now do that easily using the following command:

```
$ sudo dpkg -r caffe2
```

Testing the Caffe2 Python API

We have now installed Caffe2, but we need to make sure it is correctly installed and that its Python API is working. An easy way to do that is to return to your home directory and check whether the Python API of Caffe2 is imported and can execute correctly. This can be done using the following commands:

```
$ cd ~
$ python -c "from caffe2.python import core"
```

Do not run the preceding command from within the Caffe2 directories. This is to avoid the ambiguity of Python having to pick between your installed Caffe2 files and those in the source or build directories.

If your Caffe2 is *not* installed correctly, you may see an error of some kind, such as the one shown in the following code block, for example:

```
$ python -c "from caffe2.python import core"
Traceback (most recent call last):
 File "<string>", line 1, in <module>
ImportError: No module named caffe2.python
```

If your Caffe2 has been installed correctly, then you may not see an error. However, you may still get a warning if you don't have a GPU:

```
$ python -c "from caffe2.python import core"
WARNING:root:This caffe2 python run does not have GPU support. Will run in
CPU only mode.
```

Testing the Caffe2 C++ API

We have now installed Caffe2, but we need to make sure it is correctly installed and that its C++ API is working. An easy way to do that is to create a small C++ program that initializes the global environment of Caffe2. This is done by calling a method named `GlobalInit` and passing it the program's arguments. This is typically the first call in a Caffe2 C++ application.

Create a C++ source file named `ch1.cpp` with this code:

```
// ch1.cpp
#include "caffe2/core/init.h"

int main(int argc, char** argv)
{
    caffe2::GlobalInit(&argc, &argv);
    return 0;
}
```

We can compile this C++ source file using the following command:

```
$ g++ ch1.cpp -lcaffe2
```

We ask the linker to link with the `libcaffe2.so` shared library file by using the `-lcaffe2` option. The compiler uses the default include file locations, and the linker uses the default shared library file locations, so we do not need to specify those.

By default, Caffe2 header files are installed to a `caffe2` subdirectory in `/usr/local/include`. This location is usually automatically included in a C++ compilation. Similarly, the Caffe2 shared library files are installed to `/usr/local/lib` by default. If you installed Caffe2 to a different location, you would need to specify the include directory location using the `-I` option and the shared library file location using the `-L` option.

We can now execute the compiled binary:

```
$ ./a.out
```

If it executes successfully, then your Caffe2 installation is fine. You are now ready to write Caffe2 C++ applications.

Summary

Congratulations! This chapter provided a brief introduction to deep learning and Caffe2. We examined the process of building and installing Caffe2 on our system. We are now ready to explore the world of deep learning by building our own networks, training our own models, and using them for inference on real-world problems.

In the next chapter, we will learn about Caffe2 operators and learn how to compose them to build simple computation graphs. We will then proceed to build a neural network that can recognize handwritten digits.

Composing Networks 2

In this chapter, we will learn about Caffe2 operators and how we can compose networks using these operators. To learn how to use operators, we will start off by building a simple computation graph from scratch. After that, we will solve a real computer vision problem called MNIST (by building a genuine neural network with trained parameters) and use it for inference.

This chapter covers the following topics:

- Introduction to Caffe2 operators
- The difference between operators and layers
- How to use operators to compose a network
- Introduction to the MNIST problem
- Composing a network for the MNIST problem
- Inference through a Caffe2 network

Operators

In Caffe2, a neural network can be thought of as a directed graph, where the nodes are operators and the edges represent the flow of data between operators. Operators are the basic units of computation in a Caffe2 network. Every operator is defined with a certain number of inputs and a certain number of outputs. When the operator is executed, it reads its inputs, performs the computation it is associated with, and writes the results to its outputs.

To obtain the best possible performance, Caffe2 operators are typically implemented in C++ for execution on CPUs and implemented in CUDA for execution on GPUs. All operators in Caffe2 are derived from a common interface. You can see this common interface defined in the `caffe2/proto/caffe2.proto` file in the Caffe2 source code.

The following is the Caffe2 operator interface found in my `caffe2.proto` file:

```
// Operator Definition
message OperatorDef {
  repeated string input = 1; // the name of the input blobs
  repeated string output = 2; // the name of output top blobs
  optional string name = 3; // the operator name. This is optional.
  // the operator type. This is needed to create the object from the
  //operator
  // registry.
  optional string type = 4;
  repeated Argument arg = 5;

  // The device option that the operator should run under.
  optional DeviceOption device_option = 6;

  // Optionally, one can specify an engine when there are multiple
  // implementations available simultaneously for one device type.
  // If one specifies an engine but that engine does not exist in the
  //compiled
  // Caffe2 binary, Caffe2 will fall back to the default engine of that
  //device
  // type.
  optional string engine = 7;

  // Additional 'fake' inputs used for expressing control dependencies
  // in the operator graph. This can be used to ensure that an
  // operator does not run until another operator is ready, for e.g.
  // scheduling control. These are not passed as actual inputs to the
  // Operator implementation, and are only used by the Net class for
  // scheduling purposes.
  repeated string control_input = 8;

  // is_gradient_op argument is only used as a hint in shape inference
  // and has no runtime significance
  optional bool is_gradient_op = 9 [0,1][default = false];

  // debug information associated with the construction of the
  //operator.
  // This is an optional string with no assumed characteristics as
  // operators can be constructed in any language.
  optional string debug_info = 10;
}
```

The preceding code snippet is a definition in the **Google Protocol Buffers (ProtoBuf)** format. ProtoBuf is used by applications that need a mechanism to serialize and deserialize structured data. ProtoBuf's serialization and deserialization mechanisms are supported in most popular languages and across most popular platforms. Caffe2 uses ProtoBuf so that all of its structures, such as operators and networks, can be accessed easily through many programming languages, across different operating systems and CPU architectures.

From the preceding operator definition, we can see that an operator in Caffe2 is defined to have `input` and, `output` blobs and has a `name`, a `type`, a `device` that it executes on (such as CPU or GPU), an execution `engine`, and other information.

One of the compelling features of Caffe2 is that it has a large collection of hundreds of operators that are already defined and optimized for you. The advantage of this is that you have a large catalog of operators to compose your own networks with and there is a high probability that networks you borrow from elsewhere will be supported fully in Caffe2. This reduces the need for you to define your own operators. You can find a comprehensive list of Caffe2 operators and their documentation in the Caffe2 operators catalog at `https://caffe2.ai/docs/operators-catalogue.html`.

Example – the MatMul operator

As an example of a Caffe2 operator, consider the **MatMul** operator, which can be used to perform **matrix multiplication**. This linear algebra operation is hugely important in deep learning and lies at the heart of the implementation of important types of neural network layers, such as fully connected and convolution layers. (We will study these layers later in this chapter and in `Chapter 3`, *Training Networks*, respectively.) The matrix multiplication operation is depicted in Figure 2.1:

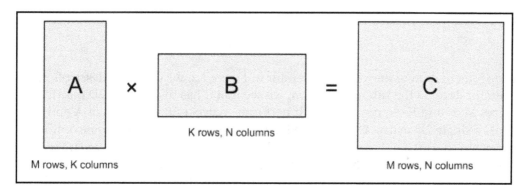

Figure 2.1: Matrix multiplication

If we look up the MatMul operator in the Caffe2 operators catalog, we find the documentation shown in Figure 2.2:

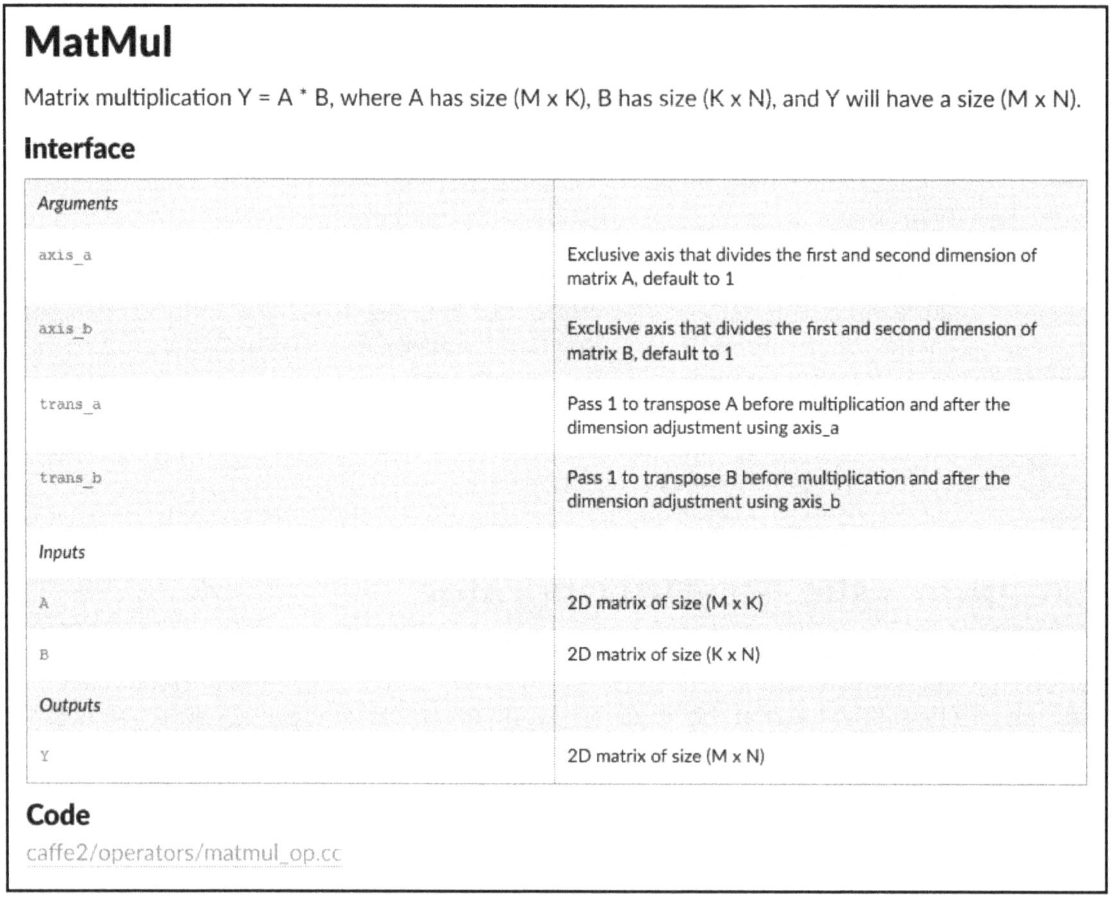

MatMul

Matrix multiplication Y = A * B, where A has size (M x K), B has size (K x N), and Y will have a size (M x N).

Interface

Arguments	
axis_a	Exclusive axis that divides the first and second dimension of matrix A, default to 1
axis_b	Exclusive axis that divides the first and second dimension of matrix B, default to 1
trans_a	Pass 1 to transpose A before multiplication and after the dimension adjustment using axis_a
trans_b	Pass 1 to transpose B before multiplication and after the dimension adjustment using axis_b
Inputs	
A	2D matrix of size (M x K)
B	2D matrix of size (K x N)
Outputs	
Y	2D matrix of size (M x N)

Code

caffe2/operators/matmul_op.cc

Figure 2.2: Documentation of the MatMul operator in Caffe2

In the documentation of the MatMul operator in *Figure 2.2*, we can see a description of what the operator does. In the **Interface** section, we see that it has two inputs: 2D matrices **A** and **B**, of sizes M×K and K×N, respectively. It performs matrix multiplication of A and B, and produces a single 2D matrix **C**, of size M×N. We can also see that it has some optional arguments to specify if either or both A and B have an exclusive axis and are transposed matrices. Finally, we also see that the Caffe2 documentation helpfully points us to the actual C++ source code that defines the MatMul operator. The documentation of all operators in Caffe2 has the following useful structure: definition, inputs, outputs, optional arguments, and a pointer to the source code.

Having learned the definition of the `MatMul` operator, here is a code snippet to create a model and add a `MatMul` operator to it:

```
model = model_helper.ModelHelper("MatMul model")
model.net.MatMul(["A", "B"], "C")
```

In the preceding code, we first create a model named `"MatMul model"` using the `ModelHelper` class of the Caffe2 `model_helper` module. A **model** is the structure used to hold a network, and the **network** is a directed graph of operators. `model_helper` is a high-level Caffe2 Python module, and its `ModelHelper` class can be used to create and manage models easily. The `model` object we created previously holds a network definition in its `net` member.

We add a `MatMul` operator to this model by calling the `MatMul` method on the model's network definition. Note the two arguments to the `MatMul` operator. The first argument is a list consisting of the names of the two matrices that need to be multiplied. Here, `"A"` and `"B"` are the names of blobs that hold the matrix elements in the Caffe2 workspace. (We will learn about the Caffe2 workspace later in this chapter.) Similarly, the second argument, `"C"`, indicates the output matrix blob in the workspace.

Difference between layers and operators

Older deep learning frameworks, such as Caffe, did not have operators. Instead, their basic units of computation were called **layers**. These older frameworks chose the name *layer* inspired by the layers in neural networks.

However, contemporary frameworks, such as Caffe2, TensorFlow, and PyTorch, prefer to use the term *operator* for their basic units of computation. There is a subtle difference between operators and layers. A layer in older frameworks, such as Caffe, was composed of both the computation function of that layer and the trained parameters of that layer. In contrast to this, an operator in Caffe2 only holds the computation function. Both the trained parameters and the inputs are external to the operator and need to be fed to it explicitly.

Example – a fully connected operator

To illustrate the difference between layers and operators, consider the **fully connected** (**FC**) operator in Caffe2. The fully connected layer is the most traditional layer in neural networks. Early neural networks were mostly composed of an input layer, one or more fully connected layers, and an output layer:

FC

Computes the result of passing an input vector X into a fully connected layer with 2D weight matrix W and 1D bias vector b. That is, the layer computes Y = X * W^T + b, where X has size (M x K), W has size (N x K), b has size (N), and Y has size (M x N), where M is often the batch size. NOTE: X does not need to explicitly be a 2D vector; rather, it will be coerced into one. For an arbitrary n-dimensional tensor X \in [a_0, a_1, ...,a_{k-1}, a_k, ..., a_{n-1}] where a_i \in N+ and k is the axis provided, then X will be coerced into a 2-dimensional tensor with dimensions [a_0 * ... * a_{k-1}, a_k * ... * a_{n-1}]. For the default case where axis=1, this means the X tensor will be coerced into a 2D tensor of dimensions [a_0, a_1 * ... * a_{n-1}], where a_0 is often the batch size. In this situation, we must have a_0 = M and a_1 * ... * a_{n-1} = K. Lastly, even though b is a 1D vector of size N, it is copied/resized to be size (M x N) implicitly and added to each vector in the batch. Each of these dimensions must be matched correctly, or else the operator will throw errors.

Interface

Arguments	
axis	(int32_t) default to 1; describes the axis of the inputs; defaults to one because the 0th axis most likely describes the batch_size
axis_w	(int32_t) default to 1; describes the axis of the weight matrix W; defaults to one because the 0th axis most likely describes the batch_size
float16_compute	Whether to use float-16 compute kernel
Inputs	
X	input tensor that's coerced into a 2D matrix of size (MxK) as described above
W	A tensor that is coerced into a 2D blob of size (KxN) containing fully connected weight matrix
b	1D blob containing bias vector
Outputs	
Y	2D output tensor

Code

caffe2/operators/fully_connected_op.cc

Figure 2.3: Interface documentation of the FC operator from the Caffe2 operators' catalog

Input **X** to an FC operator is expected to be of size M×K. Here, M is the batch size. This means that if we fed 10 different inputs to the neural network as a **batch**, M would be the batch size value, 10. Hence, each input actually appears as a vector of size 1×K to this operator. We can see that, unlike the `MatMul` operator introduced earlier, which had no trained parameters, the FC operator has inputs that are trained parameters: **W** and **b**. The trained parameter **W** is a 2D matrix of size K×N of weight values, and the trained parameter **b** is a 1D vector of bias values. The FC operator computes the output **Y** as X×W+b. This means that each input vector of size 1×K produces an output of size 1×N after being processed by this operator. And indeed, this explains the fully connected layer's name: each of the 1×K inputs is fully connected to each of the 1×N outputs:

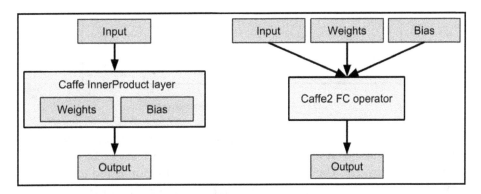

Figure 2.4: Difference between the Caffe layer and the Caffe2 operator

In older frameworks such as Caffe, the weight and bias trained parameters of the fully connected layer were stored along with the layer. In contrast, in Caffe2, the FC operator does not store any parameters. Both the trained parameters and the inputs are fed to the operator. *Figure 2.4* shows the difference between a Caffe layer and Caffe2 operator, using the fully connected layer as an example. Since most deep learning literature still refers to these entities as layers, we will use the words *layer* and *operator* interchangeably throughout the rest of this book.

Building a computation graph

In this section, we will learn how to build a network in Caffe2 using `model_helper`. (`model_helper` was introduced earlier in this chapter.) To maintain the simplicity of this example, we use mathematical operators that require no trained parameters. So, our network is a computation graph rather than a neural network because it has no trained parameters that were learned from training data. The network we will build is illustrated by the graph shown in Figure 2.5:

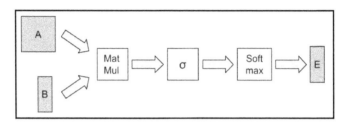

Figure 2.5: Our simple computation graph with three operators

As you can see, we provide two inputs to the network: a matrix, **A**, and a vector, **B**. A `MatMul` operator is applied to **A** and **B** and its result is fed to a `Sigmoid` function, designated by **σ** in Figure 2.5. The result of the `Sigmoid` function is fed to a `SoftMax` function. (We will learn a bit more about the `Sigmoid` and `SoftMax` operators next in this section.) Output **E** of the `Sigmoid` function is the output of the network.

Here is the Python code to build the preceding graph, feed it inputs, and obtain its output:

```
#!/usr/bin/env python2

"""Create a network that performs some mathematical operations.
Run inference on this network."""

from caffe2.python import workspace, model_helper
import numpy as np

# Initialize Caffe2
workspace.GlobalInit(["caffe2",])

# Initialize a model with the name "Math model"
model = model_helper.ModelHelper("Math model")

# Add a matrix multiplication operator to the model.
# This operator takes blobs "A" and "B" as inputs and produces blob "C" as
output.
model.net.MatMul(["A", "B"], "C")
```

```
# Add a Sigmoid operator to the model.
# This operator takes blob "C" as input and produces blob "D" as output.
model.net.Sigmoid("C", "D")

# Add a Softmax operator to the model.
# This operator takes blob "D" as input and produces blob "E" as output.
model.net.Softmax("D", "E", axis=0)

# Create input A, a 3x3 matrix initialized with some values
A = np.linspace(-0.4, 0.4, num=9, dtype=np.float32).reshape(3, 3)

# Create input B, a 3x1 matrix initialized with some values
B = np.linspace(0.01, 0.03, num=3, dtype=np.float32).reshape(3, 1)

# Feed A and B to the Caffe2 workspace as blobs.
# Provide names "A" and "B" for these blobs.
workspace.FeedBlob("A", A)
workspace.FeedBlob("B", B)

# Run the network inside the Caffe2 workspace.
workspace.RunNetOnce(model.net)

# Extract blob "E" from the workspace.
E = workspace.FetchBlob("E")

# Print inputs A and B and final output E
print A
print B
print E
```

This program can be broken down into four stages:

1. Initializing Caffe2
2. Composing the model network
3. Adding input blobs to the workspace
4. Running the model's network in the workspace and obtaining the output

You could use a similar structure in your own programs that compose a network and use it for inference.

Let's examine the Python code of each of these stages in detail.

Initializing Caffe2

Before we call any Caffe2 methods, we need to import the Caffe2 Python modules that we might need:

1. First, import the `workspace` and `module_helper` modules:

   ```
   from caffe2.python import workspace, model_helper
   import numpy as np
   ```

   This step also imports the `numpy` module so that we can create matrices and vectors easily in our program. **NumPy** is a popular Python library that provides multi-dimensional arrays (including vectors and matrices) and a large collection of mathematical operations that can be applied to such arrays.

2. Next, initialize the default Caffe2 workspace using this call:

   ```
   workspace.GlobalInit(["caffe2",])
   ```

The workspace is where all the data is created, read from, and written to in Caffe2. This means that we will use the workspace to load our inputs, the trained parameters of our network, intermediate results between operators, and the final outputs from our network. We also use the workspace to execute our network during inference.

 We created the default workspace of Caffe2 earlier. We could create other workspaces with unique names too. For example, to create a second workspace and switch to it, execute the following code:
`workspace.SwitchWorkspace("Second Workspace", True)`

Composing the model network

1. We use the `ModelHelper` class (described earlier in this chapter) to create an empty model name it `Math model`:

   ```
   # Initialize a model with the name "Math model"
   model = model_helper.ModelHelper("Math model")
   ```

2. Next, we add our first operator, `MatMul`, to the network of this model:

```
# Add a matrix multiplication operator to the model.
# This operator takes blobs "A" and "B" as inputs and produces blob
"C" as output.
model.net.MatMul(["A", "B"], "C")
```

The `MatMul` operator was described earlier in this chapter. We indicate the names of the input blobs `["A", "B"]` and output blob `"C"` in the call. A **blob** is an N-dimensional array with a name, and it holds values of the same type. For example, we could represent a matrix of floating point values as a two-dimensional blob. A blob differs from most Python data structures, such as `list` and `dict`, because all the values in it have to be of the same data type (such as `float` or `int`). All input data, output data, and trained parameters used in neural networks are stored as blobs in Caffe2.

 We have not yet created these blobs in the workspace. We are adding the operator to the network and informing Caffe2 that blobs of these names will be available in the workspace by the time the network is actually used.

3. After that, we add our next operator, `Sigmoid`, to the network:

```
# Add a Sigmoid operator to the model.
# This operator takes blob "C" as input and produces blob "D" as
output.
model.net.Sigmoid("C", "D")
```

Sigmoid operator

The `Sigmoid` operator implements the **Sigmoid function**. This function is popular in neural networks, and is also known as the **logistic function**. It is defined as follows:

$$f(x) = \frac{1}{1 + e^{-x}}$$

Figure 2.6 shows a plot of this function:

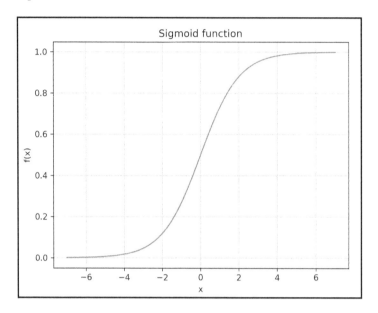

Figure 2.6: A plot of the Sigmoid function

Sigmoid is a non-linear function that is typically used in neural networks as an activation function. An **activation function** is a common layer that is introduced between one or more sequences of layers. It converts its input into an activation, which decides whether a neuron in the following layer is activated (or fired) or not. Activation functions typically introduce non-linear characteristics into a network.

Note how the Sigmoid looks like the letter S. It looks like a smoothed step function, and its outputs are bounded by 0 and 1. So, for example, it could be used to classify any input value to determine whether it belongs to a class (value **1.0**) or not (value **0.0**).

The Sigmoid function in Caffe2 is an **elementwise operator**. This means that it is applied individually to each element of the input. In our preceding code snippet, we are informing Caffe2 that this operator that we added to the network will take an input blob of name "C" from the workspace and write its output to blob "D" in the workspace.

As a final and third operator, we add the Softmax operator to the network:

```
# Add a Softmax operator to the model.
# This operator takes blob "D" as input and produces blob "E" as
output.
model.net.Softmax("D", "E", axis=0)
```

Softmax operator

The Softmax operator implements the **SoftMax function**. This function takes a vector as input and normalizes the elements of the vector in a probability distribution. It is defined on each element of a vector as follows:

$$f(x_i) = \frac{e^{x_i}}{\sum e^{x_i}}$$

The output values of a SoftMax function have nice properties. Every output value x_i is bounded by $[0, 1]$, and all the values of the output vector total 1. Due to these characteristics, this function is typically used as the last layer in a neural network used for classification.

In the preceding code snippet, we added a Softmax operator to the network that will use a blob named "D" as input and write output to a blob named "E". The axis parameter is used to indicate the axis along which the input N-dimensional array is split apart and coerced into a 2D array. Typically, axis=1 is used to indicate that the first axis of the blob is the batch dimension and that the rest should be coerced into a vector. Since we are using a single input in our example, we use axis=0 here to indicate that the entire input should be coerced into a 1D vector for Softmax.

Adding input blobs to the workspace

Our model is now ready. We now initialize our two input blobs, A and B, to this model to a linear distribution of values using NumPy:

```
# Create input A, a 3x3 matrix initialized with some values
A = np.linspace(-0.4, 0.4, num=9, dtype=np.float32).reshape(3, 3)

# Create input B, a 3x1 matrix initialized with some values
B = np.linspace(0.01, 0.03, num=3, dtype=np.float32).reshape(3, 1)
```

Note how we are specifying that all the values in these arrays will be of the floating point data type. This is indicated in NumPy using np.float32. The NumPy reshape function is used to convert the one-dimensional array of values into matrices of sizes 3×3, and 3×1, respectively.

Since we will perform inference on the network in Caffe2, we need to set the input blobs into the workspace. **Inference** is the act of passing inputs to a trained neural network and *inferring,* or obtaining, the output from it. The act of setting a blob into the workspace with a name and its values is called **feeding** in Caffe2.

Feeding our input blobs is executed using `FeedBlob` calls, shown as follows:

```
# Feed A and B to the Caffe2 workspace as blobs.
# Provide names "A" and "B" for these blobs.
workspace.FeedBlob("A", A)
workspace.FeedBlob("B", B)
```

In the preceding code snippet, we fed tensors A and B into our workspace and named those blobs "A" and "B" respectively.

Running the network

We built a network and we have its inputs ready in the workspace. We are now ready to perform inference on the network. In Caffe2, this is called a **run**. We perform a run on the network in the workspace as follows:

```
# Run the network inside the Caffe2 workspace.
workspace.RunNetOnce(model.net)
```

After the run is done, we can extract or fetch the output blob from the workspace and print our input and output blobs for reference:

```
# Extract blob "E" from the workspace.
E = workspace.FetchBlob("E")

# Print inputs A and B and final output E
print A
print B
print E
```

When this computation graph code is executed, it should produce an output like the following:

```
$ ./computation_graph.py
A: [[-0.4 -0.3 -0.2]
 [-0.1  0.   0.1]
 [ 0.2  0.3  0.4]]
B: [[0.01]
 [0.02]
 [0.03]]
```

```
E: [[0.3318345 ]
   [0.33333108]
   [0.33483443]]
```

You can work through the matrix multiplication, Sigmoid, and SoftMax layers of this graph with inputs A and B and see that E does indeed have the correct output values.

Building a multilayer perceptron neural network

In this section, we introduce the MNIST problem and learn how to build a **MultiLayer Perceptron (MLP)** network using Caffe2 to solve it. We also learn how to load pretrained parameters into the network and use it for inference.

MNIST problem

The **MNIST problem** is a classic image classification problem that used to be popular in machine learning. State-of-the-art methods can now achieve greater than 99% accuracy in relation to this problem, so it is no longer relevant. However, it acts as a stepping stone for us to learn how to build a Caffe2 network that solves a real machine learning problem.

The MNIST problem lies in identifying the handwritten digit that is present in a grayscale image of size 28 x 28 pixels. These images are from the MNIST database, a modified version of a scanned document dataset that was originally shared by the **National Institute of Standards and Technology (NIST)**, hence the name **modified NIST (MNIST)**. Examples from this dataset are shown in Figure 2.7:

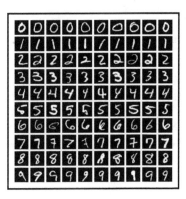

Figure 2.7: A random sample of 10 images each digit from 0 to 9, in the MNIST dataset

Note how some of the handwritten digits could be difficult for even humans to classify.

Every image in the MNIST dataset contains a single handwritten digit, between 0 and 9. The grayscale values in each image are normalized and the handwritten digit is centered in the image. This makes MNIST a good dataset for beginners since we do not need to do any image cleaning, preprocessing, or augmentation operations before using it for inference or training. (Such operations are typically required if we are using other image datasets.) Typically, 60,000 images from this dataset are used as training data, and a separate set of 10,000 images is used for testing.

Building a MNIST MLP network

To solve the MNIST problem, we will create a neural network known as a **MultiLayer Perceptron** (**MLP**). This is the classic name given to neural networks that have an input layer, an output layer, and one or more hidden layers between them. An MLP is a type of **feedforward neural network** because its network is a **directed acyclic graph** (**DAG**); that is, it does not have cycles.

The Python code to create the MLP network described in this section, to load pretrained parameters into it, and use it for inference, can be found in the `mnist_mlp.py` file that accompanies this book. In the sections that follow, we dissect this code and try to understand it.

Initializing global constants

Our Python Caffe2 code for a MNIST MLP network begins by initializing some MNIST constants:

```
# Number of digits in MNIST
MNIST_DIGIT_NUM = 10
# Every grayscale image in MNIST is of dimensions 28x28 pixels in a single
channel
MNIST_IMG_HEIGHT = 28
MNIST_IMG_WIDTH = 28
MNIST_IMG_PIXEL_NUM = MNIST_IMG_HEIGHT * MNIST_IMG_WIDTH
```

There are 10 (`MNIST_DIGIT_NUM`) digits in the MNIST dataset (0-9) that we want to identify. And the dimensions of every MNIST image are 28 x 28 pixels (`MNIST_IMG_HEIGHT`, `MNIST_IMG_WIDTH`).

Composing network layers

The following is a diagram of the MNIST MLP network we will build:

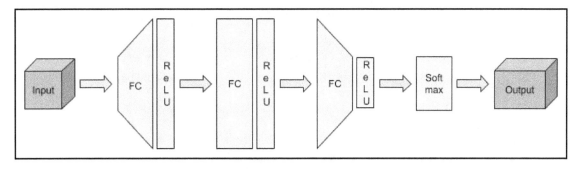

Figure 2.8: Our MNIST MLP network comprising an input layer, three pairs of FC and ReLU layers, and a final SoftMax layer

We will build a simple feedforward neural network composed of three pairs of fully connected layers and ReLU activation layers. Each pair of layers is connected to the output of its previous pair of layers. The output of the third pair of fully connected and ReLU activation layers is passed through a SoftMax layer to get the output classification values of the network. This network structure is depicted in Figure 2.8.

To build this network, we first initialize a model using `ModelHelper`, just like in our earlier computation graph example. We then use the **Brew** API to add the layers of the network.

> While using raw operator calls as in our computation graph example is possible, using Brew is far more preferable if we are building real neural networks. This is because the `helper` functions in Brew make it very easy to initialize parameters for each layer and pick a device for each layer. Doing the same using operator methods would require multiple calls with several parameters.

A typical call to a Brew `helper` function to add a layer would require these parameters:

- A model containing the network where we are adding this layer
- The name of the input blob or previous layer
- The name of this layer
- The dimensions of input to this layer
- The dimensions of output from this layer

We begin by adding the first pair of fully connected and ReLU layers using the following code:

```
# Create first pair of fullyconnected and ReLU activation layers
# This FC layer is of size (MNIST_IMG_PIXEL_NUM * 2)
# On its input side it is fed the MNIST_IMG_PIXEL_NUM pixels
# On its output side it is connected to a ReLU layer
fc_layer_0_input_dims = MNIST_IMG_PIXEL_NUM
fc_layer_0_output_dims = MNIST_IMG_PIXEL_NUM * 2
fc_layer_0 = brew.fc(
    model,
    input_blob_name,
    "fc_layer_0",
    dim_in=fc_layer_0_input_dims,
    dim_out=fc_layer_0_output_dims
)
relu_layer_0 = brew.relu(model, fc_layer_0, "relu_layer_0")
```

Notice that, in this pair of layers, the input is of the `MNIST_IMG_PIXEL_NUM` dimensions, and the output is of the `MNIST_IMG_PIXEL_NUM * 2` dimensions.

ReLU layer

The following figure shows the ReLU function:

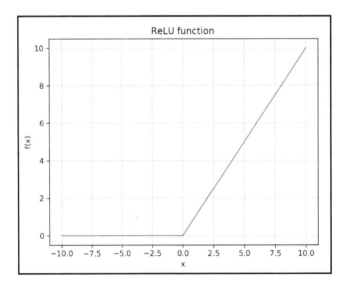

Figure 2.9: The ReLU function

We introduced an activation layer called Sigmoid while building the computation graph. Here, we use another popular activation layer called **Rectified Linear Unit (ReLU)**. This function can be seen in *Figure 2.9*, and is defined as follows:

$$f(x) = \begin{cases} 0, \text{if } x < 0 \\ x, \text{otherwise} \end{cases}$$

We add a second and a third pair of layers named ("fc_layer_1", "relu_layer_1") and ("fc_layer_2", "relu_layer_2"), respectively, using the following code:

```
# Create second pair of fullyconnected and ReLU activation layers
fc_layer_1_input_dims = fc_layer_0_output_dims
fc_layer_1_output_dims = MNIST_IMG_PIXEL_NUM * 2
fc_layer_1 = brew.fc(
    model,
    relu_layer_0,
    "fc_layer_1",
    dim_in=fc_layer_1_input_dims,
    dim_out=fc_layer_1_output_dims
)
relu_layer_1 = brew.relu(model, fc_layer_1, "relu_layer_1")
# Create third pair of fullyconnected and ReLU activation layers
fc_layer_2_input_dims = fc_layer_1_output_dims
fc_layer_2_output_dims = MNIST_IMG_PIXEL_NUM
fc_layer_2 = brew.fc(
    model,
    relu_layer_1,
    "fc_layer_2",
    dim_in=fc_layer_2_input_dims,
    dim_out=fc_layer_2_output_dims
)
relu_layer_2 = brew.relu(model, fc_layer_2, "relu_layer_2")
```

The second pair takes in MNIST_IMG_PIXEL_NUM * 2-sized input and outputs MNIST_IMG_PIXEL_NUM * 2. The third pair takes in MNIST_IMG_PIXEL_NUM * 2 and outputs MNIST_IMG_PIXEL_NUM.

When solving a classification problem using a neural network, we typically need a probability distribution over the classes. We add a SoftMax layer to the end of our network to achieve this:

```
# Create a softmax layer to provide output probabilities for each of
# 10 digits. The digit with highest probability value is considered to be
# the prediction of the network.
softmax_layer = brew.softmax(model, relu_layer_2, "softmax_layer")
```

Notice how the `brew.softmax` method does not need to be told the input and output dimensions explicitly when that information can be obtained from the input it is connected to. This is one of the advantages of using Brew methods.

Set weights of network layers

After composing the network, we now incorporate the pretrained weights of the layers into the network. These weights were obtained by training this network on the MNIST training data. We will learn how to train a network in the next chapter. In this chapter, we focus on loading those pretrained weights into our network and performing inference.

Note that, of the three types of layer we use in this network, only the fully connected layers need pretrained weights. We have stored the weights as NumPy files for ease of loading. They can be loaded from disk using the NumPy `load` method. These values are set in the workspace using the `workspace.FeedBlob` method by specifying the layer name to which they belong.

The code snippet to achieve this is as follows:

```
for i, layer_blob_name in enumerate(inference_model.params):
    layer_weights_filepath = "mnist_mlp_weights/{}.npy".format(str(i))
    layer_weights = np.load(layer_weights_filepath, allow_pickle=False)
    workspace.FeedBlob(layer_blob_name, layer_weights)
```

Running the network

So we have built a network and we have initialized its layers with pretrained weights. We are now ready to feed it input and execute an inference through the network to get its output.

We could feed input images one by one to our network and obtain the output classification results. However, doing this in production systems would not utilize the computation resources of the CPU or GPU effectively and would result in a low throughput for inference. So, almost all deep learning frameworks allow users to feed a batch of input data to a network, for both inference and training purposes.

To illustrate feeding a batch of input images, we have the `mnist_data.npy` file, which holds the data for a batch of 64 MNIST images. We read this batch from the file and set it as the data blob in the workspace so that it acts as the input to the network:

```
# Read MNIST images from file to use as input
input_blob = None
with open("mnist_data.npy") as in_file:
    input_blob = np.load(in_file)
# Set MNIST image data as input data
workspace.FeedBlob("data", input_blob)
```

We execute inference on the network by calling the `workspace.RunNetOnce` method with the network as input:

```
workspace.RunNetOnce(inference_model.net)
```

We fetch the output blob of the network from the workspace and, for each of the 64 inputs, we determine which MNIST digit class has the highest confidence value; that is what the network believes was the digit in the MNIST image:

```
network_output = workspace.FetchBlob("softmax_layer")
for i in range(len(network_output)):
    # Get prediction and confidence by finding max value and its index
    # in preds array
    prediction, confidence = max(enumerate(network_output[i]),
    key=operator.itemgetter(1))
    print("Input: {} Prediction: {} Confidence: {}".format(i,
    prediction, confidence)
```

When we execute this script, we obtain outputs like the following:

```
Input: 0 Prediction: 5 Confidence: 0.609326720238
Input: 1 Prediction: 7 Confidence: 0.99536550045
Input: 2 Prediction: 9 Confidence: 0.877566576004
Input: 3 Prediction: 9 Confidence: 0.741059184074
Input: 4 Prediction: 2 Confidence: 0.794860899448
Input: 5 Prediction: 0 Confidence: 0.987336695194
Input: 6 Prediction: 7 Confidence: 0.900308787823
Input: 7 Prediction: 1 Confidence: 0.993218839169
Input: 8 Prediction: 6 Confidence: 0.612009465694
```

This means that the network thinks that the first input image had the digit 5, the second one had 7, and so on.

Summary

In this chapter, we learned about Caffe2 operators and how they differ from layers used in older deep learning frameworks. We built a simple computation graph by composing several operators. We then tackled the MNIST machine learning problem and built an MLP network using Brew helper functions. We loaded pretrained weights into this network and used it for inference on a batch of input images. We also introduced several common layers, such as matrix multiplication, fully connected, Sigmoid, SoftMax, and ReLU.

We learned about performing inference on our networks in this chapter. In the next chapter, we will learn about training and how to train a network to solve the MNIST problem.

3
Training Networks

In *Chapter 2*, *Composing Networks*, we learned how to create Caffe2 operators and how we can compose networks from them. In this chapter, the focus is on training neural networks. We will learn how to create a network that is intended for training and how to train it using Caffe2. We will continue to use the MNIST dataset as an example. However, instead of the MLP network we built in the previous chapter, we will create a popular network named LeNet.

This chapter will cover the following topics:

- Introduction to training a neural network
- Building the training network for LeNet
- Training and monitoring the LeNet network

Introduction to training

In this section, we provide a brief overview of how a neural network is trained. This will help us to understand the later sections where we use Caffe2 to actually train a network.

Components of a neural network

We employ neural networks to solve a particular type of problem for which devising a computer algorithm would be onerous or difficult. For example, in the MNIST problem (introduced in *Chapter 2*, *Composing Networks*), handcrafting a complicated algorithm to detect the common stroke patterns for each digit, and thereby determining each digit, would be tedious. Instead, it is easier to design a neural network suited to this problem and then train it (as shown later in this chapter) using a lot of data to do the same. If the training data is diverse and the training is done carefully, such a network would also be far more robust to variations in the input data than any deterministic handcrafted algorithm would.

A neural network has two main components: its structure and its weights. We typically design the network structure and then use a training algorithm and training data to determine the weights. After it is trained, the network structure, with its embedded weights, can be used for inference on new unseen data, as shown in the following diagram:

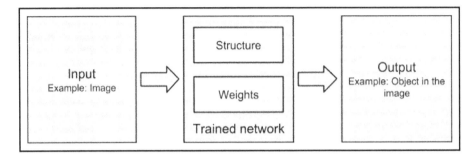

Figure 3.1: Structure and weights of a network used for inference

Structure of a neural network

The structure of a network is the series of its layers, their types, and their configurations. The structure is typically devised by a researcher or a practitioner familiar with the problem that the neural network is being designed to solve. For example, to solve image classification problems, computer vision researchers might typically use a series of convolution layers in the network. (We will learn about the convolution layer later in this chapter.) Various configuration parameters of each layer also need to be determined beforehand, such as the size and number of the convolution filters in a convolution layer. There is a huge amount of interest in using deep learning itself to ascertain the structure of a network suited to a particular problem. However, discussion of this meta-learning topic is beyond the scope of this book.

Weights of a neural network

The second component of a network is its weights and biases. We generally refer to them together as **weights**, or sometimes as **parameters**. These are the floating point values that are the parameters of every layer in the network. How the weights of a layer are used is determined by the type of layer. For example, in a fully connected layer, a bigger weight value might signify a stronger correlation between an input signal and the network's output. In a convolution layer, the weights of a convolution filter might signify what type of pattern or shape in the input it is looking for.

In summary, we sit down and devise the structure of a network to solve a particular problem. Our choices in this process will be limited by our understanding of the problem space, the types of layers available in the DL framework, the hardware constraints of the accelerator we are using, and how much training time we are prepared to put up with. For example, the memory available in a GPU or CPU might limit the number of weights we might use in a layer or the number of layers we might use in the network. The amount of training time we are willing to spend also limits the number of weights and layers we can use in a network, because the more of these we employ, the longer it may take for the network to converge and train.

Training process

Once we have a network structure fleshed out, we can then use a DL framework such as Caffe2 to describe that structure. We then apply one of the many training algorithms available in the framework on our training data. This trains the network and learns the weights of the layers that would best amplify the signal and dampen the noise. This process is depicted in Figure 3.2:

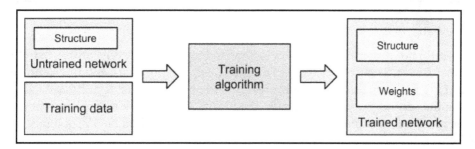

Figure 3.2: Training is the process of learning the weights of a neural network using a training algorithm and data

Neural networks are typically trained using a gradient-based optimization algorithm. To do this, we first define an **objective function** or **loss function** for the network. This function computes a loss or error value by comparing the output of the network on a given input to the ground truth result of that input. The training process iteratively picks training data and computes its loss, and then uses the optimization algorithm to update the weights so that the error is reduced. This process is repeated until we see no further improvement in the accuracy of the network:

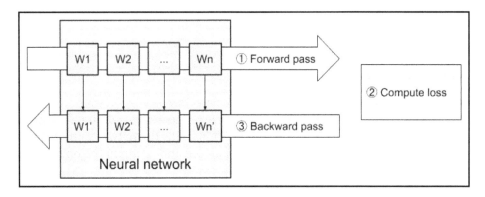

Figure 3.3: Three stages of an iteration in training

A single iteration of the training process is depicted in *Figure 3.3*. We can see that it has three distinct stages. The first stage is a **Forward pass**, where we essentially perform inference of the network with its current weights to obtain the result or hypothesis of the network. In the second stage, we compute the loss of the network using a loss function. The third stage is a **Backward pass**, where we use an algorithm called backpropagation to update the weights of the network.

Gradient descent variants

There are commonly three variants of gradient descent we can employ to sample the training data used in every iteration of training. If we use the entire training dataset in each iteration, this process is called **batch gradient descent**. If we use one randomly chosen sample of the training data in each iteration, then the process is called **stochastic gradient descent**. The variant that is most commonly used is **mini-batch gradient descent**, where we use a randomly chosen subset of the training data in each iteration. For best results, this is done by shuffling the training data, and then dividing it into mini-batches used in each iteration. After we are finished with one run through the training data, called an **epoch**, we shuffle and divide again into batches and continue.

In the remainder of this chapter, we will learn about the LeNet network that can be used for MNIST, how to build it, and how to use it for training using Caffe2.

LeNet network

In `Chapter` 2, *Composing Networks*, we built an MLP network that was composed of multiple pairs of fully connected layers and activation layers. In this chapter, we will build and train a **convolutional neural network** (**CNN**). This type of network is so named because it primarily uses convolution layers (introduced in the next section). For computer vision problems, CNNs have been shown to deliver better results with fewer numbers of parameters compared to MLPs. One of the first successful CNNs was used to solve the MNIST problem that we looked at earlier. This network, named **LeNet-5**, was created by Yann LeCun and his colleagues:

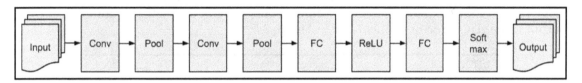

Figure 3.4: Structure of our LeNet model

We will construct a network similar in spirit to the LeNet. We will refer to this as the LeNet model in the remainder of this book. From *Figure 3.4*, we can see that our LeNet network has eight layers. After the input layer, there are two pairs of convolution layers and pooling layers. They are followed by a pair of fully connected and ReLU activation layers and another fully connected layer. A final SoftMax layer is used to obtain the MNIST classification result.

We next look at two new layers that are important in CNNs and are part of LeNet: convolution and pooling.

Convolution layer

The *convolution layer* is the most important layer in neural networks that are used to solve computer vision problems, involving images and video. The input tensor to a convolution layer has at least three dimensions in its size: $C \times H \times W$. That is, the input has C channels, each channel being a 2D matrix of height H and width W. This follows naturally from the layout of images. For example, an RGB image has three channels, each channel of a certain height and width.

When we refer to **convolution**, we generally mean **2-dimensional** (**2D**) convolution. A 2D convolution layer has two sets of parameters that are learned during training: filter parameters and bias parameters.

The first set of parameters associated with a 2D convolution layer is K filters. Each **filter** or **kernel** is a **3-dimensional** (**3D**) tensor of shape $C \times R \times S$ holding floating point values that were learned during training. So, the total number of filter parameters that need to be learned during training for a 2D convolution layer is $K \times C \times R \times S$. Note how a kernel of a 2D convolution layer has the same number of channels, C, as the input to the layer.

The second set of parameters associated with a 2D convolution layer are K bias values, each value being associated with each of the K filters described previously.

During convolution, each of the K kernels is slid across the width and height of the input. At every location where a kernel stops, a dot product is computed between the kernel values and the input values that overlap with the kernel, in order to obtain one output value for that location. Finally, the bias value associated with that kernel is added to each output value. This process is illustrated in Figure 3.5:

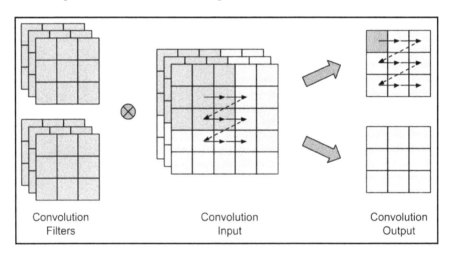

Figure 3.5: 2D convolution of $3 \times 5 \times 5$ input with two filters of shape $3 \times 3 \times 3$. Output is of the shape $2 \times 3 \times 3$

Note how convolving with each kernel results in an output tensor of size $H' \times W'$. Thus, when an input of size $C \times H \times W$ is fed to a 2D convolution layer, the resulting output is of size $K \times H' \times W'$. If we feed a batch of N inputs to a 2D convolution layer, the resulting output is of size $N \times K \times H' \times W'$.

A 2D convolution layer has a few other arguments. A couple of important arguments are the stride and padding. **Stride** indicates how many values along the height and width a kernel moves before stopping to perform a convolution. For example, if the stride is 2×2, kernels only visit every alternate location in the input. **Padding** indicates how much the height and width of input can be assumed to be expanded with **padding values** for performing convolution. Zero values are commonly used as padding values, and this is called **zero padding**.

Pooling layer

Another popular type of layer used in CNNs is called the **pooling layer**. It is typically used to reduce the width and height of the outputs of a previous layer. It operates by subsampling its input to produce the output. Unlike a convolution layer, a pooling layer does not have any pretrained parameters. It has two arguments associated with it: a **window size** and a **reduction function**. Similar to the convolution layer, a pooling layer has arguments such as stride and padding.

What the pooling layer does is to slide the window of specified width and height across the input. At each location where it stops, it applies its reduction function to the input values in the window to produce a single output value:

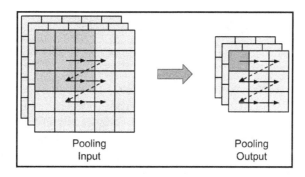

Figure 3.6: Pooling layer producing $3 \times 3 \times 3$ output after pooling $3 \times 5 \times 5$ input with a 3×3 pooling window

Common reduction functions are max and average. In a max-pooling layer, the maximum of the values in the input window becomes the output value. In an **average-pooling layer**, the average of the values in the input window becomes the output value. *Figure 3.6* illustrates an operation in a max-pooling layer.

The pooling window is 2D and moves along the width and height of the input. So, it only reduces the width and height of the input. The number of channels remains the same in the input and in the output.

We are now ready to look at a code example that trains a LeNet network. The complete source code for this is available as `ch3/mnist_lenet.py`. We begin by reading the MNIST training data in the next section.

Training data

We use brew in this chapter to simplify the process of building our LeNet network. We begin by first initializing the model using `ModelHelper`, which was introduced in the previous chapter:

```
# Create the model helper for the train model
train_model = model_helper.ModelHelper(name="mnist_lenet_train_model")
```

We then add inputs to the training network using our `add_model_inputs` method:

```
# Specify the input is from the train lmdb
data, label = add_model_inputs(
    train_model,
    batch_size=64,
    db=os.path.join(data_folder, "mnist-train-nchw-lmdb"),
    db_type="lmdb",
)
```

Training data is usually stored in a **database (DB)** so that it can be accessed efficiently. Reading from a DB is usually faster than reading from thousands of individual files on the filesystem. For every training image in the MNIST dataset, the DB stores the 28×28 grayscale pixel values of the image and the digit that is in the image. Each grayscale pixel value is an 8-bit unsigned integer, with values in the range $[0, 255]$. The actual digit that is in each image is called a **label** and is usually annotated by a human by inspecting the image. For example, if the handwritten digit in the image is a 9, then a human annotator would have looked at the image and given it a label of 9.

In our `add_model_inputs` method, we use a convenient brew helper function named `db_input` to connect the DB to our model:

```
# Load data from DB
input_images_uint8, input_labels = brew.db_input(
    model,
    blobs_out=["input_images_uint8", "input_labels"],
    batch_size=batch_size,
```

```
        db=db,
        db_type=db_type,
    )
```

We specify the names of the blobs in our workspace to which the image and label data should be stored: `input_images_uint8` and `input_labels`. We also specify the batch size and information required to access the DB, such as its name and type.

Neural networks almost always work with float values, ideally normalized to the range $[0, 1]$. So, we indicate that our input image data, which is an 8-bit unsigned integer data type, should be cast to the float data type and normalized:

```
# Cast grayscale pixel values to float
# Scale pixel values to [0, 1]
input_images = model.Cast(input_images_uint8, "input_images",
to=core.DataType.FLOAT)
input_images = model.Scale(input_images, input_images, scale=float(1./256))
```

Note how the Caffe2 `ModelHelper` provides helpful methods to perform both these operations with ease: `Cast` and `Scale`.

Finally, we add a `StopGradient` operator to the image data blob to indicate to the backward pass algorithm not to compute gradients for it:

```
# We do not need gradient for backward pass
# This op stops gradient computation through it
input_images = model.StopGradient(input_images, input_images)
```

We do this because the input layer is not a real layer of the neural network. It has no learnable parameters and does not have anything to be trained. So, the backward pass can stop there and does not need to move past it. `StopGradient` is a pseudo operator in Caffe2 that achieves this effect.

Building LeNet

We build the LeNet layers required for inference by calling the `build_mnist_lenet` method in our script:

```
# Build the LeNet network
softmax_layer = build_mnist_lenet(train_model, data)
```

Note how we only pass in the image pixel data input to this network and not the labels. The labels are not required for inference; they are required for training or testing to use as ground truth to compare against the prediction of the network's final layer.

The remainder of the following subsections describe how we add pairs of convolution and pooling layers, the fully connected and ReLU layers, and the final SoftMax layer, to create the LeNet network.

Layer 1 – Convolution

The first layer in LeNet is a convolution layer, which we introduced earlier in this chapter. We build it from a Caffe2 2D convolution operator, `Conv2D`, available in the operators' catalog. This can be added to the model using the handy `brew.conv` method.

When creating the operator, we specify that the input is a single-channel matrix of grayscale values. We also indicate that the output should have 20 channels, each channel holding a matrix. Finally, we specify that each convolution kernel used should have a width and height of 5 pixels. In Caffe2, we can provide minimal information like this and the API figures out the rest of the necessary arguments:

```
# Convolution layer that operates on the input MNIST image
# Input is grayscale image of size 28x28 pixels
# After convolution by 20 kernels each of size 5x5,
# output is 20 channels, each of size 24x24
layer_1_input_dims = 1   # Input to layer is grayscale, so 1 channel
layer_1_output_dims = 20 # Output from this layer has 20 channels
layer_1_kernel_dims = 5  # Each kernel is of size 1x5x5
layer_1_conv = brew.conv(
    model,
    input_blob_name,
    "layer_1_conv",
    dim_in=layer_1_input_dims,
    dim_out=layer_1_output_dims,
    kernel=layer_1_kernel_dims,
)
```

Let's expand these values to get a better idea of the sizes of the input, output, and kernels of this layer. Since the MNIST dataset is a 28×28 grid of values of a single grayscale channel, the input to this first layer of the network is a 3D array of size $1 \times 28 \times 28$. We are performing 2D convolution here, where each kernel has the same number of channels as the input to the layer. Furthermore, we indicated that the kernel width and height should be 5. So, the size of each kernel is $1 \times 5 \times 5$. Since we indicated that we want 20 channels of output from this layer, we need 20 such kernels. Hence, the actual size of kernel parameters of this layer is $20 \times 1 \times 5 \times 5$. Convolution layers also use a bias value, one for each output channel, so the size of bias values is 20×1.

If a $1 \times 5 \times 5$ kernel is convolved on a $1 \times 28 \times 28$ input with a stride of 1, the result is 24×24. When 20 such kernels are used, the result is $20 \times 24 \times 24$. This is the size of the output of this layer.

Layer 2 – Max-pooling

The output of the first convolution layer is connected to a max-pooling layer, introduced earlier in this chapter. We build it from a Caffe2 max-pooling operator, `MaxPool`, available in the operators' catalog. This can be added to the model using the handy `brew.max_pool` method. When creating this operator, we specify that its kernels are 2 x 2 in size, and that the stride is 2:

```
# Max-pooling layer that operates on output from previous convolution layer
# Input is 20 channels, each of size 24x24
# After pooling by 2x2 windows and stride of 2, the output of this layer
# is 20 channels, each of size 12x12
layer_2_kernel_dims = 2 # Max-pool over 2x2 windows
layer_2_stride = 2       # Stride by 2 pixels between each pool
layer_2_pool = brew.max_pool(
    model,
    layer_1_conv,
    "layer_2_pool",
    kernel=layer_2_kernel_dims,
    stride=layer_2_stride,
)
```

The output of the previous convolution layer was of the size $20 \times 24 \times 24$. When max-pooling using window size 2×2 and stride 2 is performed, the output is of the size $20 \times 12 \times 12$.

Layers 3 and 4 – Convolution and max-pooling

The first pair of convolution and pooling layers is followed by another pair of convolution and pooling layers in LeNet, to further reduce the width and height and increase the channels:

```
# Convolution layer that operates on output from previous pooling layer.
# Input is 20 channels, each of size 12x12
# After convolution by 50 kernels, each of size 20x5x5,
# the output is 50 channels, each of size 8x8
layer_3_input_dims = 20  # Number of input channels
layer_3_output_dims = 50 # Number of output channels
layer_3_kernel_dims = 5  # Each kernel is of size 50x5x5
layer_3_conv = brew.conv(
    model,
    layer_2_pool,
    "layer_3_conv",
    dim_in=layer_3_input_dims,
    dim_out=layer_3_output_dims,
    kernel=layer_3_kernel_dims,
)


# Max-pooling layer that operates on output from previous convolution layer
# Input is 50 channels, each of size 8x8
# Apply pooling by 2x2 windows and stride of 2
# Output is 50 channels, each of size 4x4
layer_4_kernel_dims = 2 # Max-pool over 2x2 windows
layer_4_stride = 2      # Stride by 2 pixels between each pool
layer_4_pool = brew.max_pool(
    model,
    layer_3_conv,
    "layer_4_pool",
    kernel=layer_4_kernel_dims,
    stride=layer_4_stride,
)
```

The second pair of convolution and pooling layers is similar to the first pair, in that convolution kernels have a size of 5 x 5 and the stride is 2, while the max-pooling window size is 2×2 and the stride is 2. What is different is that the second convolution layer uses 50 kernels to produce an output having 50 channels. After the second convolution layer, the output is of the size $50 \times 8 \times 8$. After the second max-pooling layer, the output is $50 \times 4 \times 4$. Note how the width and height of the inputs have gone down dramatically.

Layers 5 and 6 – Fully connected and ReLU

The convolution and pooling layers are followed by a pair of fully connected and ReLU layers, added using the handy methods, `brew.fc` and `brew.relu`:

```
# Fully-connected layer that operates on output from previous pooling layer
# Input is 50 channels, each of size 4x4
# Output is vector of size 500
layer_5_input_dims = 50 * 4 * 4
layer_5_output_dims = 500
layer_5_fc = brew.fc(
    model,
    layer_4_pool,
    "layer_5_fc",
    dim_in=layer_5_input_dims,
    dim_out=layer_5_output_dims,
)

# ReLU layer that operates on output from previous fully-connected layer
# Input and output are both of size 500
layer_6_relu = brew.relu(
    model,
    layer_5_fc,
    "layer_6_relu",
)
```

The input to the fully connected layer is of size $50 \times 4 \times 4$. This 3D input is flattened to a vector of size 800 when fed to the fully connected layer. We have specified the output size of the layer as 500. So this layer needs to learn 800×500 values, plus a bias value, during training, so that they can be used during inference. The output of the fully connected layer is fed to a ReLu layer, which acts as an activation function.

Layer 7 and 8 – Fully connected and Softmax

LeNet-5 uses a second fully connected layer to reduce the output down to the 10 values required to predict probabilities for the 10 digits:

```
# Fully-connected layer that operates on output from previous ReLU layer
# Input is of size 500
# Output is of size 10, the number of classes in MNIST dataset
layer_7_input_dims = 500
layer_7_output_dims = 10
layer_7_fc = brew.fc(
    model,
    layer_6_relu,
```

```
    "layer_7_fc",
    dim_in=layer_7_input_dims,
    dim_out=layer_7_output_dims,
)
```

A final SoftMax layer converts the 10 output values of the fully connected layer to a probability distribution:

```
# Softmax layer that operates on output from previous fully-connected layer
# Input and output are both of size 10
# Each output (0 to 9) is a probability score on that digit
layer_8_softmax = brew.softmax(
    model,
    layer_7_fc,
    "softmax",
)
```

Training layers

In earlier sections, we built the layers of a LeNet network required for inference and added inputs of image pixels and the label corresponding to each image. In this section, we are adding a few layers at the end of the network required to compute the loss function and for backpropagation. These layers are only required during training and can be discarded when using the trained network for inference.

Loss layer

As we noted in the *Introduction to training* section, we need a `loss` function at the end of the network to determine the error of the network. Caffe2 provides implementations of many common loss functions as operators in its operators' catalog.

For this example, we compute the loss value using **categorical cross-entropy loss**. This loss is typically used to measure the performance of a classification model whose output is between 0 and 1. In Caffe2, this loss can be implemented as a composition of two operators, `LabelCrossEntropy` and `AveragedLoss`, shown as follows:

```
# Compute cross entropy between softmax scores and labels
cross_entropy = train_model.LabelCrossEntropy([softmax_layer, label],
"cross_entropy")

# Compute the expected loss
loss = train_model.AveragedLoss(cross_entropy, "loss")
```

Optimization layers

In the *Introduction to training* section, we noted how a gradient-based optimization algorithm lies at the heart of the training process.

We first indicate to Caffe2 to use the output of the loss layer we added earlier to start the computation of gradients during the backward pass during training:

```
# Use the average loss we just computed to add gradient operators to the
model
train_model.AddGradientOperators([loss])
```

The `AddGradientOperators` method takes away the pain of specifying these operators explicitly and adds them to the network for us.

Finally, we specify the gradient-based optimization algorithm **Stochastic Gradient Descent (SGD)** to be used for our training:

```
# Specify the optimization algorithm
optimizer.build_sgd(
    train_model,
    base_learning_rate=0.1,
    policy="step",
    stepsize=1,
    gamma=0.999,
)
```

We specify important SGD parameters, such as the learning rate to use, the policy to use in order to change the learning rate, the step size, and gamma.

Optimization algorithms are implemented as `Optimizer` in Caffe2. The DL framework has implementations of many common optimization algorithms, including SGD, Adam, AdaGrad, RMSProp, and AdaDelta. In our preceding call, we used a helpful wrapper, `build_sgd`, provided by the `optimizer` module that configures the SGD optimizer for us.

Accuracy layer

Finally, we indicate that the accuracy of the model should be tracked with a call to our `add_accuracy_op` method, which has this statement:

```
brew.accuracy(model, [softmax_layer, label], "accuracy")
```

Note the second argument to the function call. This indicates to Caffe2 that the output of the SoftMax layer should be compared against the ground truth labels to determine the accuracy of the model.

The `accuracy` layer is helpful for human supervision of the training process. We can perform inference at any point in the training process and, using the output of the accuracy layer, get a sense of how accurate the network is at that point.

Training and monitoring

We begin the training process by creating the network in the workspace and initializing all the parameter blobs of the network in the workspace. This is done by calling the workspace `RunNetOnce` method:

```
# The parameter initialization network only needs to be run once.
workspace.RunNetOnce(train_model.param_init_net)
```

Next, we ask Caffe2 to create the network in memory:

```
# Creating an actual network as a C++ object in memory.
# We need this as the object is going to be used a lot
# so we avoid creating an object every single time it is used.
workspace.CreateNet(train_model.net, overwrite=True)
```

We are finally ready to train. We iterate a predetermined number of times and, in each iteration, we use the workspace `RunNet` method to run a forward pass and a backward pass.

Training a small network such as our LeNet model is fast both on CPU and GPU. However, many of the real models you train might take several hours or days to train. For this reason, it is a good idea to constantly monitor the training process by extracting the loss and accuracy after every training iteration.

For our LeNet model, we use the following code to extract the loss and accuracy values after each training iteration from the output blobs of the loss and accuracy layers we added earlier to the training network:

```
# Run the network for some iterations and track its loss and accuracy
total_iters = 100
accuracy = np.zeros(total_iters)
loss = np.zeros(total_iters)
for i in range(total_iters):
    workspace.RunNet(train_model.net)
    accuracy[i] = workspace.blobs["accuracy"]
    loss[i] = workspace.blobs["loss"]
```

```
print("Iteration: {}, Loss: {}, Accuracy: {}".format(i, loss[i],
accuracy[i]))
```

We can monitor the health of the training by looking at the raw values, or importing them into a spreadsheet, or plotting them in a graph. Figure 3.7 shows a graph plotted from the values of one such training session:

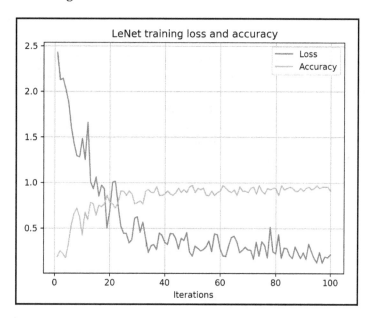

Figure 3.7: Loss and accuracy of training our model

We can see that the loss is high at the beginning. This is expected, as we typically initialize a network with zero or random weights. As the training proceeds, we see that the loss decreases and, correspondingly, the accuracy of the network increases. If you do not see the loss decreasing or accuracy increasing, then that indicates a problem with our training parameters or training data. If the training pace is slow or is causing values to blow off, then you might need to tweak the learning rate and such parameters.

We can typically stop training at any iteration where the loss curve is leveling off and the accuracy is suitable. To aid the export of a model at a particular iteration, it is a good idea to export the model to disk (demonstrated in Chapter 5, *Working with Other Frameworks*) after each iteration. That way, you can pick the model at the best iteration after the training is complete.

Another useful practice is to measure the accuracy on a validation dataset after every epoch or so. **Validation data** is typically a portion of the training data that is separated out for this purpose prior to the training. We did not use validation data in our example, in order to keep it simple.

Summary

In this chapter, we learned about the general training process for a neural network using a gradient-based optimization algorithm. We learned about CNNs and the classic LeNet CNN to solve the MNIST problem. We built this network, and learned how to add training and test layers to it, so that we could use it for training. We finally used this network to train and learned how to monitor the network during training using Caffe2. In the following chapters, we will learn how to work with models trained using other frameworks, such as Caffe, TensorFlow, and PyTorch.

4
Working with Caffe

In Chapter 2, *Composing Networks*, and Chapter 3, *Training Networks*, we learned how to compose networks and train them, respectively. In this chapter, we will examine the relationship between Caffe2 and Caffe and look at how to use Caffe models in Caffe2 and vice versa.

The objectives of this chapter are as follows:

- The relationship between Caffe and Caffe2
- Introduction to AlexNet
- Building and installing Caffe
- Caffe model file formats
- Caffe2 model file formats
- Converting a Caffe model to Caffe2
- Converting a Caffe2 model to Caffe

The relationship between Caffe and Caffe2

At the *NIPS* academic conference held in 2012, Alex Krizhevsky and his collaborators, one of whom was the neural network pioneer, Geoffrey Hinton, presented a record breaking result at the **ImageNet Large-Scale Visual Recognition Competition** (**ILSVRC**). Research teams competed in various image recognition tasks that used the ImageNet dataset. Krizhevsky's results on the image classification task were 10.8% better than the state of the art. He had used GPUs for the first time to train a CNN with many layers. This network structure would popularly be called **AlexNet** later. The design of such a deep neural network with a large number of layers is the reason why this field came to be called deep learning. Krizhevsky shared the entire source code of his network, now called **cuda-convnet**, along with its highly GPU-optimized training code.

Soon after this, **Yangqing Jia**, and his collaborators from the UC **Berkeley Vision and Learning Center** (**BVLC**) tried to replicate these results, releasing their software as *DeCaf*. This library was later polished and streamlined and released as **Caffe**.

Unlike most of the buggy and poorly designed research code of its time, Caffe was a well-designed deep learning library that made it easy to compose a network using a prototxt text file. It was modular by design, making it easy for researchers to add new layers and training algorithms. This made Caffe popular during the period 2012 to 2016. Most of the groundbreaking networks and models in the field of image recognition were released in Caffe. This is why Caffe is an important deep learning framework, and you might still find several classic models only available for Caffe.

In the meantime, there was growing interest in alternatives to Caffe. This was because Caffe was beginning to show its limitations. Although a Python API was added late in 2014, Caffe was primarily a C++ library. This C++ requirement meant slow speed of experimentation and development. Caffe was also primarily designed for image recognition problems. Practitioners found it difficult to add features for solving other problems, such as speech recognition. Other useful features, such as the utilization of different precision data types and quantization and multi-GPU training, were not present in Caffe. These features were later grafted painfully onto Caffe, but were not optimal in terms of engineering and maintenance.

These issues resulted in a new breed of deep learning libraries that were written with ease of use, distributed training, and customization in mind, gaining in popularity. These included TensorFlow and PyTorch.

Yangqing Jia moved from university to Facebook and he led the creation of a modern deep learning library, Caffe2, the subject of this book. Because he had created Caffe too, Caffe2 borrowed a lot of the good ideas from Caffe and was built to interoperate with Caffe.

Introduction to AlexNet

We mentioned AlexNet in the earlier section that introduced Caffe. AlexNet was a seminal network structure because of the large number of layers it employed for the first time, and for showing how such a deep neural network could be trained in a reasonable time by utilizing GPUs.

Figure 4.1 shows the network structure of AlexNet generated by Caffe's network visualization tool, `draw_net.py` . This tool uses the GraphViz library to render the graph layout:

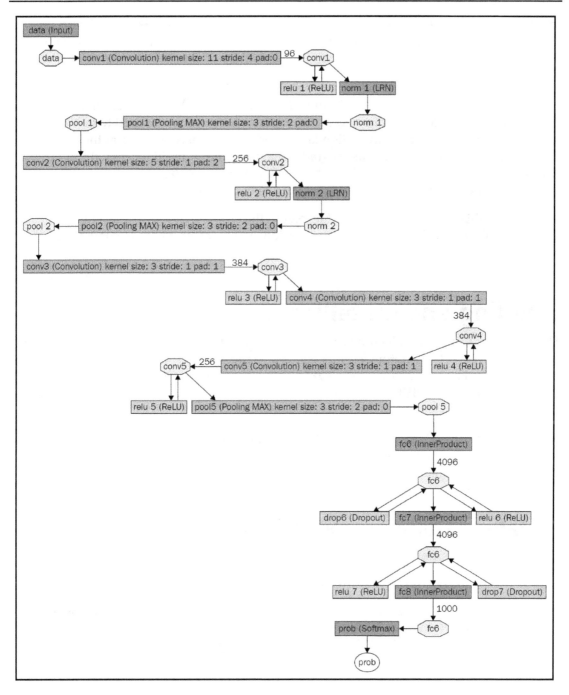

Figure 4.1: Network structure of AlexNet using the GraphViz layout

In this visualization, layers are drawn as rectangles and data tensors between layers are drawn as elongated octagons. For example, the first layer rectangle after the input layer depicts a convolution layer named `conv1`. It uses kernels of size 11×11, a stride of 4, and a padding of 0.

Examining the AlexNet structure in *Figure 4.1* we can see that AlexNet is similar in spirit to the LeNet model we looked at in `Chapter 3`, *Training Networks*. Compared to LeNet, however, it has many more convolution layers and fully connected layers at the end. Furthermore, it has replaced the use of traditional tanh and sigmoid layers with ReLU. Krizhevsky describes in his paper how these changes, along with some training innovations and the use of GPUs, made training such a deep network tractable.

In the rest of this chapter, we will use AlexNet as the example model to learn how to understand Caffe and Caffe2 network description languages, and how to convert between the two.

Building and installing Caffe

The version of Caffe maintained by BVLC can be freely downloaded from `https://github.com/BVLC/caffe`. A GPU-optimized fork of Caffe maintained by NVIDIA can be downloaded from `https://github.com/NVIDIA/caffe`. For the remainder of this discussion, we will use BVLC Caffe, though NVIDIA Caffe should also build and work similarly.

Note that Caffe offers building using CMake or Make. We look at the CMake build process in this book. If you want Caffe to use the GPU, you will need to have CUDA and cuDNN libraries already installed.

Installing Caffe prerequisites

Install the following prerequisites:

1. First, install the libraries that Caffe depends on:

```
$ sudo apt install libboost-all-dev libprotobuf-dev libleveldb-dev
libsnappy-dev libopencv-dev libhdf5-serial-dev protobuf-compiler
libgflags-dev libgoogle-glog-dev liblmdb-dev
```

2. For BLAS on CPU, the best performance comes from installing Intel's MKL libraries. (Steps to install MKL were described in `Chapter 1`, *Introduction and Installation*.) If you do not have MKL, or you are not using an Intel CPU, then you can install either ATLAS or OpenBLAS:

```
$ sudo apt install libatlas-base-dev libopenblas-dev
```

3. To build the Python interface to Caffe, make sure these packages are installed:

```
$ sudo apt install libboost-python-dev python-skimage python-protobuf
```

We are now ready to build Caffe from source.

Building Caffe

To build Caffe, observe the following steps:

1. Since we have chosen to use CMake, the building process is simple and straightforward:

```
$ mkdir build
$ cd build
$ cmake ..
$ make
```

2. To build and run the Caffe unit tests, execute the following command:

```
$ make runtest
```

 This can take a substantial amount of time to finish.

3. To build the Python interface to Caffe, execute the following command:

```
$ make pycaffe
$ make install
```

4. By default, the install directory will be a subdirectory inside the `build` directory. Add this `build/install/python` path to the `PYTHONPATH` environment variable before you import Caffe into Python.

Caffe model file formats

To be able to use Caffe models in Caffe2, we first need to understand the model file formats that Caffe can export to. Caffe exports a trained model into two files, as follows:

1. The structure of the neural network is stored as a `.prototxt` file
2. The weights of the layers of the neural network are stored as a `.caffemodel` file

Prototxt file

The prototxt is a text file that holds information about the structure of the neural network:

- A list of layers in the neural network
- The parameters of each layer, such as its name, type, input dimensions, and output dimensions
- The connections between the layers

Caffe exports a neural network by serializing it using the Google **Protocol Buffers** (**ProtoBuf**) serialization library. The prototxt file is a serialization of the neural network structure in the ProtoBuf text format.

We can look at the prototxt files of some of the popular CNN networks in the `models` directory in the Caffe source code. (Refer to the *Building and Installing Caffe* section on how to get Caffe source code.) You might find several prototxt filenames there, each of which has a different purpose.

Here is a description of what some of the typical Caffe prototxt filenames mean:

- `deploy.prototxt`: This file describes the structure of the network that can be deployed for inference. It does not include the extra layers that are typically required for training a network. (We looked at extra layers or operators added to network for training in `Chapter 3`, *Training Networks*.) This is the prototxt file we typically want, if we wish to take a pretrained Caffe model and use it for inference in Caffe2.
- `train_val.prototxt`: This file describes the structure of the network that was used for training. It includes all the extra layers that were added to aid in the training and validation process. This is the prototxt file we typically want, if we wish to take a pretrained Caffe model and continue training or fine-tuning it in Caffe2.

Now, let's look at AlexNet as an example. (AlexNet was introduced earlier in this chapter.) A version of the AlexNet pretrained model is available in the Caffe source code in the `models/bvlc_alexnet` directory.

Here are the first two layers from the `deploy.prototxt` file of AlexNet:

```
$ head -26 models/bvlc_alexnet/deploy.prototxt
name: "AlexNet"
layer {
  name: "data"
  type: "Input"
  top: "data"
  input_param { shape: { dim: 10 dim: 3 dim: 227 dim: 227 } }
}
layer {
  name: "conv1"
  type: "Convolution"
  bottom: "data"
  top: "conv1"
  param {
    lr_mult: 1
    decay_mult: 1
  }
  param {
    lr_mult: 2
    decay_mult: 0
  }
  convolution_param {
    num_output: 96
    kernel_size: 11
    stride: 4
  }
}
```

We can see that the `prototxt` file format is easy to read and modify by humans. Note that the network is named `"AlexNet"`. We can see two layers in the preceding code snippet named `"data"` and `"conv1"`. The `"data"` layer is an `Input` layer and we can see that it requires input to be of dimensions $10 \times 3 \times 227 \times 227$. The `"conv1"` layer is a `Convolution` layer and we can see many of its parameters, including a kernel size of 11×11 and stride of size 4×4.

The syntax used for describing a neural network as a Caffe prototxt file is, itself, described in a `caffe.proto` text file. This is a file written in the Google protocol buffer language. You can find this file in the Caffe source code at `src/caffe/proto/caffe.proto`.

As an example, here is a partial description of `ConvolutionParameter` from the `caffe.proto` file:

```
message ConvolutionParameter {
  optional uint32 num_output = 1; // The number of outputs for the layer
  optional bool bias_term = 2 [default = true]; // whether to have bias
  //terms

  // Pad, kernel size, and stride are all given as a single value for equal
  // dimensions in all spatial dimensions, or once per spatial dimension.
  repeated uint32 pad = 3; // The padding size; defaults to 0
  repeated uint32 kernel_size = 4; // The kernel size
  repeated uint32 stride = 6; // The stride; defaults to 1
  optional uint32 pad_h = 9 [default = 0]; // The padding height (2D only)
  optional uint32 pad_w = 10 [default = 0]; // The padding width (2D only)

  optional uint32 group = 5 [default = 1]; // The group size for group conv

  // ... Omitted other details.
  // ... Find all details in caffe.proto
}
```

By looking at this, we can start to understand the convolution layer parameters in the `deploy.prototxt` easily, for example, what the parameters `num_outputs`, `kernel_size`, and `stride` mean.

In this way, you can understand any Caffe prototxt file that you come across. It is essentially a list of layers, with names and parameters and links to previous and later layers. For information about a particular layer type, refer to the `caffe.proto` file.

Caffemodel file

The `caffemodel` file is a binary file that holds the weights of the layers of a neural network. This file is a serialization of the trained neural network in the **ProtoBuf binary format**. A binary format is used because of the need to store floating point or integer values that represent the weights. This file is typically large, in the order of hundreds of megabytes, and so it typically needs to be downloaded separately.

For each of the popular models that Caffe provides along with its source code, there is a corresponding `readme.md` file that has the details required to download the `caffemodel` file for that network. As an example, Figure 4.2 shows the `readme.md` of the AlexNet model:

```
---
name: BAIR/BVLC AlexNet Model
caffemodel: bvlc_alexnet.caffemodel
caffemodel_url: http://dl.caffe.berkeleyvision.org/bvlc_alexnet.caffemodel
license: unrestricted
sha1: 9116a64c0fbe4459d18f4bb6b56d647b63920377
caffe_commit: 709dc15af4a06bebda027c1eb2b3f3e3375d5077
---

This model is a replication of the model described in the [AlexNet](
http://papers.nips.cc/paper/4824-imagenet-classification-with-deep-convolutional-neural-networks)
 publication.

Differences:
- not training with the relighting data-augmentation;
- initializing non-zero biases to 0.1 instead of 1 (found necessary for training, as
initialization to 1 gave flat loss).

The bundled model is the iteration 360,000 snapshot.
The best validation performance during training was iteration 358,000 with validation accuracy
57.258% and loss 1.83948.
This model obtains a top-1 accuracy 57.1% and a top-5 accuracy 80.2% on the validation set,
using just the center crop.
(Using the average of 10 crops, (4 + 1 center) * 2 mirror, should obtain a bit higher accuracy.)

This model was trained by Evan Shelhamer @shelhamer

## License

This model is released for unrestricted use.
```

Figure 4.2: readme.md of the AlexNet model

Downloading Caffe model files

Caffe provides a Python script in `scripts/download_model_binary.py` in its source code that can be used to download the caffemodel files of a model. This script needs to be provided with the model directory as input. For example, to download the `caffemodel` file for AlexNet, we can invoke the following command:

```
$ python scripts/download_model_binary.py models/bvlc_alexnet/
```

This script looks for a `readme.md` in the input model directory (like the one in *Figure 4.2*), figures out the caffemodel URL from the preamble in the `readme.md`, downloads the `caffemodel` file, and ensures that the downloaded file is correct by matching its SHA1 hash to the hash provided in the preamble.

Caffe2 model file formats

To be able to use Caffe models in Caffe2, we also need to understand the model file formats that Caffe2 can import. Just like Caffe, Caffe2 also uses Protobuf for serialization and deserialization of its model files. Caffe2 imports a trained model from two files:

1. The structure of the neural network stored as a `predict_net.pb` file or as a `predict_net.pbtxt` file
2. The weights of the operators of the neural network stored as a `init_net.pb` file

predict_net file

The `predict_net` binary file, which is usually named `predict_net.pb`, holds the list of operators in the neural network, the parameters of each operator, and the connections between the operators. This file is a serialization of the neural network structure in the ProtoBuf binary format.

We can observe that Caffe2 uses a binary serialization file compared to a text serialization file used by Caffe. This is not too much trouble in Caffe2 because it has a Python API that can be used to easily understand the network structure after importing the file.

Optionally, we can also use `predict_net` text file, usually named `predict_net.pbtxt`, which is a text file that is equivalent to the `predict_net` binary file, but stored in the ProtoBuf text format.

Continuing with our AlexNet example, the first convolution layer of that network would appear as a convolution operator in `predict_net.pbtxt`, shown as follows:

```
name: "AlexNet"
op {
  input: "data"
  input: "conv1_w"
  input: "conv1_b"
  output: "conv1"
  type: "Conv"
  arg {
    name: "stride"
    i: 4
  }
  arg {
    name: "pad"
    i: 0
  }
```

```
  arg {
    name: "kernel"
    i: 11
  }
}
```

Note how the `predict_net` text file is quite easy for humans to read, just like the prototxt text file of Caffe.

The syntax used for describing a neural network as a Caffe2 `predict_net` file is itself described in a `caffe2.proto` text file. This is a file written in the Google protocol buffer language. You can find this file in the Caffe2 source code at `proto/caffe2.proto`.

Here is the definition of the operator from `caffe2.proto`:

```
// Operator Definition.
message OperatorDef {
  repeated string input = 1; // the name of the input blobs
  repeated string output = 2; // the name of output top blobs
  optional string name = 3; // the operator name. This is optional.
  // the operator type. This is needed to create the object from the
  //operator
  // registry.
  optional string type = 4;
  repeated Argument arg = 5;

  // The device option that the operator should run under.
  optional DeviceOption device_option = 6;

  // Optionally, one can specify an engine when there are multiple
  // implementations available simultaneously for one device type.
  // If one specifies an engine but that engine does not exist in the
  //compiled
  // Caffe2 binary, Caffe2 will fall back to the default engine of that
  //device
  // type.
  optional string engine = 7;

  // ... Omitted other details.
  // ... Find all details in caffe2.proto
}
```

We can see how Caffe2 defines an operator in more general terms, instead of focusing on defining each and every operator (or layer) explicitly as Caffe did.

init_net file

The `init_net binary file`, which is typically named `init_net.pb`, holds the weights of the operators of a neural network. This file is a serialization of the trained neural network in the ProtoBuf binary format. Just like the Caffe `caffemodel` file, this file too can be typically large, in the order of hundreds of megabytes. It is named `init_net` because the weights inside the file can be used to initialize the operators in the network.

Converting a Caffe model to Caffe2

To be able to use a Caffe model in Caffe2, we need to convert it from its Caffe formats to Caffe2 file formats. Caffe2 provides a script named `python/caffe_translator.py` that can be used for this purpose.

For example, we can convert our AlexNet files from Caffe to Caffe2 by invoking the script as follows:

```
$ python python/caffe_translator.py
path_to_caffe/models/bvlc_alexnet/deploy.prototxt
path_to_caffe/models/bvlc_alexnet/bvlc_alexnet.caffemodel --init_net
init_net.pb --predict_net predict_net.pb
```

Running this script generates three files, `predict_net.pb`, `predict_net.pbtxt`, and `init_net.pb`, for AlexNet:

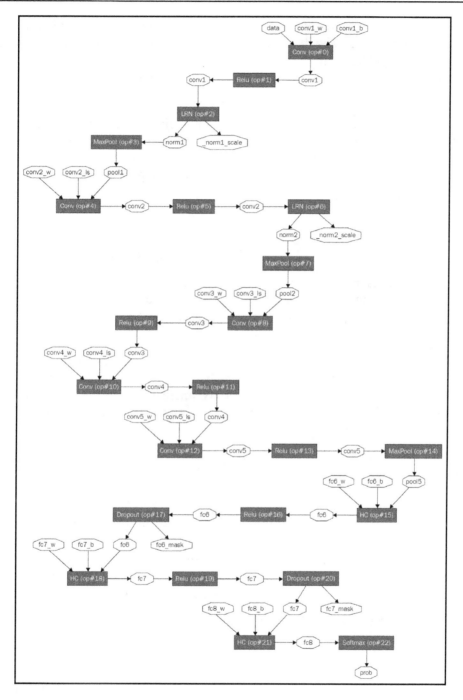

Figure 4.3: AlexNet network structure in Caffe2

Figure 4.3 shows the AlexNet network structure in Caffe2 after it was converted from the Caffe model. This graph visualization was generated using the `Caffe2 net_drawer.py` tool that utilizes GraphViz for the network layout. You can find more information about Caffe2 model visualization using `net_drawer` in `Chapter 7`, *Caffe2 at the Edge and in the cloud*.

From the diagram, we can see that every Caffe layer is replaced with a Caffe2 operator. The operators are drawn in rectangles and both weights and data tensors are drawn as elongated octagons. By looking at the first convolution operator, we note how it has three tensors—one for the data (named `data`), and two for the weights and bias for that operator (named `conv1_w` and `conv1_b`).

Converting a Caffe2 model to Caffe

In the previous sections in this chapter, we focused on how to convert a Caffe model to a Caffe2 model. Since Caffe is not being actively developed now, and Caffe2 was, in part, created to supersede Caffe2, this path of migrating a Caffe model to Caffe2 is what the majority of users are interested in.

However, if you need to use a Caffe2 model in Caffe, then that process is bound to be more arduous. There does not seem to be any direct way to convert a Caffe2 model to Caffe. If you are sure that the Caffe2 operators and their arguments are fully supported in Caffe, then you could try going through an intermediary format such as ONNX (see `Chapter 5`, *Working with Other Frameworks*).

If the ONNX route is not feasible, then you might have to resort to executing the following tasks manually:

1. Export Caffe2 operators, arguments, and weights of the model
2. Create a Caffe network manually, matching Caffe2 operators to corresponding Caffe layers
3. Implement new Caffe layers in C++ if there isn't a layer matching an operator
4. Load weights manually to Caffe layers and use this Caffe network for inference

Summary

In this chapter, we introduced the Caffe deep learning framework and examined the relationship between Caffe and Caffe2. We examined the Caffe and Caffe2 model file formats. Using AlexNet as an example network, we looked at how to convert a Caffe model to Caffe2 format. Finally, we looked at the difficulties in converting a Caffe2 model to Caffe.

Caffe is a DL framework that has reached its end of life and no new features are being added to it. In the next chapter, we will look at contemporary DL frameworks, such as TensorFlow and PyTorch, and see how we can exchange models to and from Caffe2 and these other frameworks.

5
Working with Other Frameworks

In Chapter 4, *Working with Caffe*, we learnt about Caffe and its relationship with Caffe2. We examined the Caffe and Caffe2 model file formats and looked at the process of importing a pre-trained Caffe model into Caffe2 using AlexNet as an example. In this chapter, we will look at how to export from, and import to, Caffe2 from other popular DL frameworks. And we will also look at how to enable other DL frameworks to use a model trained with Caffe2.

The topics covered in this chapter are as follows:

- The ONNX model format
- Support for ONNX in Caffe2
- How to export a Caffe2 model to ONNX format
- How to import an ONNX model into Caffe2
- How to visualize ONNX models

Open Neural Network Exchange

Open Neural Network Exchange (**ONNX**), typically pronounced as *on-niks*, is a format to represent a computation graph, with support for a wide variety of operators and data types. This format is general enough to support both neural networks and traditional ML models. Started by Facebook and Microsoft, this format has quickly gained a reputation as a popular format for the export and import of deep neural networks among most DL frameworks.

Installing ONNX

The ONNX source code can be found online at: `https://github.com/onnx/onnx` This includes definitions of the format and scripts to operate on ONNX files. Libraries and tools to convert from and to specific DL framework formats are usually provided by DL frameworks.

DL frameworks with built-in support for ONNX include Caffe2, PyTorch, MXNet, and Chainer. There are also converters to convert to and from other DL frameworks, such as TensorFlow. There are runtimes that can use ONNX models on specialized hardware accelerators. For example, TensorRT provides an inference runtime with ONNX support for use on NVIDIA GPUs, and OpenVINO does the same for use on Intel CPUs. (We will discuss TensorRT and OpenVINO in `Chapter 6`, *Deploying Models to Accelerators for Inference*.)

The Python library of ONNX can be installed easily, using the following command on Ubuntu:

```
$ sudo pip install onnx
```

You can check if the installation was successful by testing whether the following command at the shell executes successfully:

```
$ python -c "import onnx"
```

ONNX format

ONNX is an open source format and its specification and source code can be found online at `https://github.com/onnx/onnx`. In `Chapter 4`, *Working with Caffe*, we observed how both Caffe2 and Caffe use Google ProtoBuf for defining the data structure for serialization and deserialization of their network structures and weights. ONNX also uses Google ProtoBuf. It supports both ProtoBuf versions 2 and 3.

The definition of a graph, such as that of a neural network or generally any ML model, defines the various operators that the graph is composed of, the operators' parameters and the relationship between the operators. The syntax and semantics of this information are defined in ONNX as two distinct representations. The **Intermediate Representation** (**IR**) defines constructs, such as graph, node, and tensor. The operators define the various types of possible operators in the graph.

ONNX IR

The ProtoBuf definition of the ONNX computation graph and its data types can be found defined in the `onnx/onnx.in.proto` file in the ONNX source code. These are also referred to as the IR of ONNX.

By examining the IR definition of ONNX in the preceding file we can see the following definitions:

- `NodeProto`: Used to define each of the layers in a neural network or each of the nodes in other ML models.
- `ModelProto`: Used to define a model and its associated graph.
- `GraphProto`: Used to define the **directed acyclic graph** (**DAG**) structure of a neural network or the graph of other ML models.
- `TensorProto`: Used to define an N-dimensional tensor.
- `TypeProto`: Used to define the ONNX data types.

ONNX operators

The definition of an operator in ONNX can be found in the `onnx/onnx-operators.in.proto` file in the ONNX source code. We can find the definitions of `OperatorProto`, `OperatorSetProto`, and `FunctionProto` in this file.

The actual definitions of all the operators supported in ONNX can be found in C++ source files named `defs.cc` in subdirectories under the `onnx/defs` directory in the ONNX source code. For example, many of the common neural network operators can be found defined in the `onnx/defs/math/defs.cc` and `onnx/defs/nn/defs.cc` files in the ONNX source code.

For another example, consider the ReLU operator that we introduced in Chapter 3, *Training Networks*. This operator has the name `Relu` (note the lower case *lu*) in ONNX and is defined in the `onnx/defs/math/defs.cc` file in the ONNX source code as follows:

```
static const char* Relu_ver6_doc = R"DOC(
    Relu takes one input data (Tensor<T>) and produces one output data
    (Tensor<T>) where the rectified linear function, y = max(0, x), is
    applied to the tensor elementwise.
    )DOC";

ONNX_OPERATOR_SET_SCHEMA(
    Relu,
    6,
```

```
OpSchema()
    .SetDoc(Relu_ver6_doc)
    .Input(0, "X", "Input tensor", "T")
    .Output(0, "Y", "Output tensor", "T")
    .TypeConstraint(
        "T",
        {"tensor(float16)", "tensor(float)", "tensor(double)"},
        "Constrain input and output types to float tensors.")
.TypeAndShapeInferenceFunction(propagateShapeAndTypeFromFirstInput));
```

We can see that every operator is defined using the ONNX_OPERATOR_SET_SCHEMA macro. This macro is defined in the onnx/defs/schema.h source file as follows:

```
#define ONNX_OPERATOR_SET_SCHEMA(name, ver, impl) \
ONNX_OPERATOR_SET_SCHEMA_EX(name, Onnx, ONNX_DOMAIN, ver, true, impl)
```

We can see that every operator definition has three components: name (name), version (ver) and implementation (impl).

Thus, for the example of the Relu operator we saw in the preceding definition, we can deduce the following characteristics:

- **Name**: The name of the operator in ONNX. In this case, it is Relu. Note that individual DL frameworks might map this name to a distinct operator or layer name in their own DL framework. That is, the name in ONNX and the corresponding name in the DL framework may not always be the same.
- **Version**: The version of the definition of this operator. In this case, it is version 6.
- **Implementation**:
  - A documentation string explaining what the operator does. In this case, it is as follows:

"Relu takes one input data (Tensor<T>) and produces one output data (Tensor<T>) where the rectified linear function, y = max(0, x), is applied to the tensor elementwise."

  - The input operands. In this case, a single tensor.
  - The output operands. In this case, a single tensor.
  - Constraints on the data type of the tensor values. In this case, ONNX is stating that it only supports data types of float (32-bit), double (64-bit) and float16 (16-bit, sometimes called half) for tensor values.
  - A function to infer the type and shape of the tensor operands. In this case, it states that the output tensor must have the same type and shape as the input tensor. It does this by using the function named propagateShapeAndTypeFromFirstInput.

From the example of the preceding definition of the Relu operator, we can see that every operator definition has a lot of documentation embedded in it. All of this is used to auto-generate the complete ONNX operator documentation. This auto-generated documentation can be found as the `docs/Operators.md` files in the ONNX source code. This is a useful reference when we are searching for a suitable ONNX operator or trying to understand the details of a particular ONNX operator.

For example, the auto-generated documentation of the `Relu` operator that we considered previously appears as shown as follows in Figure 5.1:

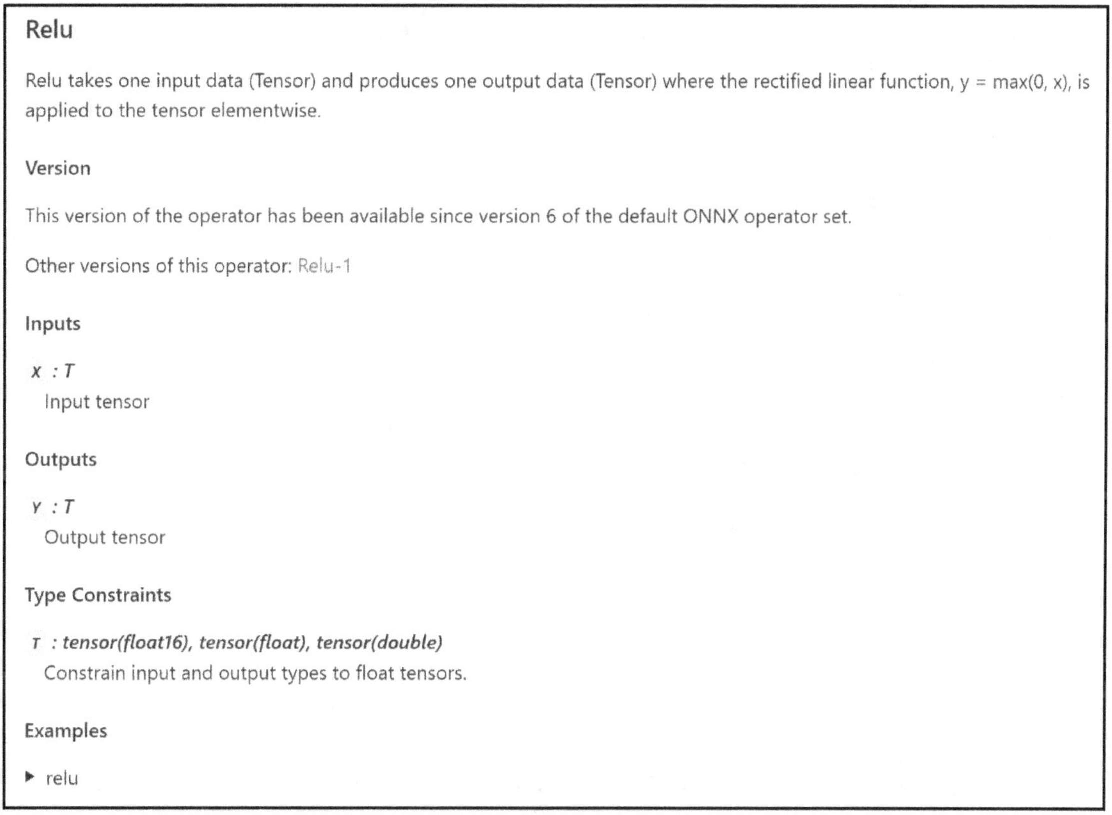

Relu

Relu takes one input data (Tensor) and produces one output data (Tensor) where the rectified linear function, y = max(0, x), is applied to the tensor elementwise.

Version

This version of the operator has been available since version 6 of the default ONNX operator set.

Other versions of this operator: Relu-1

Inputs

x : T
  Input tensor

Outputs

y : T
  Output tensor

Type Constraints

T : tensor(float16), tensor(float), tensor(double)
  Constrain input and output types to float tensors.

Examples

▶ relu

Figure 5.1: Auto-generated Relu operator documentation in ONNX

ONNX in Caffe2

Caffe2 has built-in support for ONNX. This includes support for exporting Caffe2 models to ONNX format and importing ONNX models directly for inference in Caffe2. C++ source files related to Caffe2's support of ONNX can be found in the `onnx` directory in the Caffe2 source code. Python source files that provide the frontend and backend support for ONNX can be found in the `python/onnx` directory in the Caffe2 source code.

The `onnx/onnx_exporter.h` and `onnx/onnx_exporter.cc` contain the definitions necessary to export a Caffe2 model to ONNX format. Support for exporting from Caffe2 to ONNX includes details such as the mapping from Caffe2 to ONNX for operators, data types, and transformations of data.

For example, in `onnx/onnx_exporter.cc` we find the following mapping of some Caffe2 operators to ONNX operators:

```
const std::unordered_map<std::string, std::string>&
OnnxExporter::get_renamed_operators() const {
  const static std::unordered_map<std::string, std::string>
kRenamedOperators{
      {"SpatialBN", "BatchNormalization"},
      {"Conv1D", "Conv"},
      {"Conv2D", "Conv"},
      {"Conv3D", "Conv"},
      {"ConvTranspose1D", "ConvTranspose"},
      {"ConvTranspose2D", "ConvTranspose"},
      {"ConvTranspose3D", "ConvTranspose"},
      {"MaxPool1D", "MaxPool"},
      {"MaxPool2D", "MaxPool"},
      {"MaxPool3D", "MaxPool"},
      {"AveragePool1D", "AveragePool"},
      {"AveragePool2D", "AveragePool"},
      {"AveragePool3D", "AveragePool"}};
  return kRenamedOperators;
}
```

Every DL framework that uses ONNX will have such a mapping. This is because every DL framework tends to have its own distinct operator or layer naming and a distinct jargon of defining the operator characteristics and relationships between operators. So, a clear and complete mapping is necessary for a DL framework to be able to digest an ONNX model definition into its own graph definition.

From the mapping between Caffe2 and ONNX we can see that the Caffe2 `SpatialBN` operator is renamed as the `BatchNormalization` operator in ONNX. Similarly, the Caffe2 `Conv2D` operator is renamed as the `Conv` operator in ONNX.

Exporting the Caffe2 model to ONNX

Caffe2 models can be easily exported to ONNX format using Python. This enables a vast number of other DL frameworks to use our Caffe2 models for training and inference. The frontend module provided by Caffe2-ONNX does all of the heavy lifting of the exporting. This module is located as the python/onnx/frontend.py file in the Caffe2 source code.

The ch5/export_to_onnx.py script provided along with this book's source code shows how to export an existing Caffe2 model to ONNX format. As an example, consider converting the Caffe2 model of AlexNet that we created in Chapter 4, *Working with Caffe*. We exported the operators and the weights of this network in Caffe2 to the files predict_net.pb and init_net.pb files respectively.

We can invoke the ONNX conversion script, as follows, to convert this Caffe2 model to an ONNX file named alexnet.onnx:

```
./export_to_onnx.py predict_net.pb init_net.pb alexnet.onnx
```

Let's look at the pertinent sections of this script that help us to export from Caffe2 to ONNX.

First are the imports, which are seen in the following code:

```
import onnx import caffe2.python.onnx.frontend from caffe2.proto import
caffe2_pb2
```

The caffe2.proto.caffe2_pb2 module has the functionality needed to import the Caffe2 models stored in the protobuf format. The onnx and caffe2.python.onnx.frontend modules have the functionality that's necessary to export to ONNX format.

In the following script we also define the name and shape of the inputs to the model:

```
INPUT_NAME = "data"
INPUT_SHAPE = (1, 3, 227, 227)
```

In Chapter 4, *Working with Caffe*, you might have noticed that the input layer and parameters are annotated in the Caffe protobuf format. However, this information is not stored in both the Caffe2 protobuf format and the ONNX format. We would need to explicitly indicate the name and shape of the input whenever we use a Caffe2 and ONNX model.

We used an AlexNet model in this example, which has input named `data`, and the input shape is `(1, 3, 227, 227)`. Note that not all models have this input shape. For example, popular CNN models have inputs with the shape `(1, 3, 224, 224)`.

We are now ready to read in the Caffe2 model files using the `caffe2_pb2` methods, as shown in the following example:

```
# Read Caffe2 predict and init model files to protobuf

predict_net = caffe2_pb2.NetDef()
with open(predict_net_fpath, "rb") as f:
    predict_net.ParseFromString(f.read())

init_net = caffe2_pb2.NetDef()
with open(init_net_fpath, "rb") as f:
    init_net.ParseFromString(f.read())
```

We need to read in both the `predict_net.pb` and `init_net.pb` Caffe2 model files, representing the network and its weights respectively. We do this by using the familiar `ParserFromString` method, which originates from the Google ProtoBuf Python library.

Next we should initialize the data type and tensor shape of the input and associate that information with the input name using a Python dictionary, as follows:

```
# Network input type, shape and name

data_type = onnx.TensorProto.FLOAT
value_info = {INPUT_NAME: (data_type, INPUT_SHAPE)}
```

We can now convert the Caffe2 `protobuf` objects to an ONNX `protobuf` object using the `caffe2_net_to_onnx_model` method of the `frontend` module, as follows:

```
# Convert Caffe2 model protobufs to ONNX

onnx_model = caffe2.python.onnx.frontend.caffe2_net_to_onnx_model(
    predict_net,
    init_net,
    value_info,
)
```

Note how this conversion method needs the input information, stored in `value_info`, for the conversion.

Finally, we can serialize the ONNX `protobuf` object to a byte buffer using the ProtoBuf `SerializeToString` method and then write that buffer to disk, as follows:

```
# Write ONNX protobuf to file

print("Writing ONNX model to: " + onnx_model_fpath)
with open(onnx_model_fpath, "wb") as f:
    f.write(onnx_model.SerializeToString())
```

The full source code of the `ch5/export_to_onnx.py` script is listed as follows:

```
#!/usr/bin/env python2

"""Script to convert Caffe2 model files to ONNX format.

Input is assumed to be named "data" and of dims (1, 3, 227, 227)
"""

# Std
import sys

# Ext
import onnx
import caffe2.python.onnx.frontend
from caffe2.proto import caffe2_pb2

INPUT_NAME = "data"
INPUT_SHAPE = (1, 3, 227, 227)

def main():

    # Check if user provided all required inputs
    if len(sys.argv) != 4:
        print(__doc__)
        print("Usage: " + sys.argv[0] + " <path/to/caffe2/predict_net.pb>
<path/to/caffe2/init_net.pb> <path/to/onnx_output.pb>")
        return

    predict_net_fpath = sys.argv[1]
    init_net_fpath = sys.argv[2]
    onnx_model_fpath = sys.argv[3]

    # Read Caffe2 model files to protobuf

    predict_net = caffe2_pb2.NetDef()
    with open(predict_net_fpath, "rb") as f:
        predict_net.ParseFromString(f.read())
```

```
init_net = caffe2_pb2.NetDef()
with open(init_net_fpath, "rb") as f:
    init_net.ParseFromString(f.read())

print("Input Caffe2 model name: " + predict_net.name)

# Network input type, shape and name

data_type = onnx.TensorProto.FLOAT
value_info = {INPUT_NAME: (data_type, INPUT_SHAPE)}

# Convert Caffe2 model protobufs to ONNX

onnx_model = caffe2.python.onnx.frontend.caffe2_net_to_onnx_model(
    predict_net,
    init_net,
    value_info,
)

# Write ONNX protobuf to file

print("Writing ONNX model to: " + onnx_model_fpath)
with open(onnx_model_fpath, "wb") as f:
    f.write(onnx_model.SerializeToString())


if __name__ == "__main__":
    main()
```

Using the ONNX model in Caffe2

In the previous section, we converted a Caffe2 model to ONNX format so that it could be used with other DL frameworks. In this section, we will learn how to use an ONNX model exported from other DL frameworks into Caffe2 for inference.

The backend module provided in the Caffe2 ONNX package enables this import of the ONNX model to Caffe2. This can be seen in the backend.py file in the python/onnx directory in the Caffe2 source code.

The ch5/run_onnx_model.py script provided along with this book's source code demonstrates how to load an ONNX model to Caffe2, and run an inference on an input image using that model.

The script first imports the Python modules necessary to work with the images (PIL.Image), **Caffe2**, and ONNX (caffe2.python.onnx.backend) as follows:

```
# Std
import PIL.Image
import json
import sys

# Ext
import numpy as np
from caffe2.python import workspace
import onnx
import caffe2.python.onnx.backend
```

The prepare_input_image method reads in an image from the input file path and prepares it to be passed as a blob to Caffe2, as shown in the following example:

```
def prepare_input_image(img_fpath):
    """Read and prepare input image as AlexNet input."""

    # Read input image as 3-channel 8-bit values
    pil_img = PIL.Image.open(sys.argv[1])

    # Resize to AlexNet input size
    res_img = pil_img.resize((IMG_SIZE, IMG_SIZE), PIL.Image.LANCZOS)

    # Convert to NumPy array and float values
    img = np.array(res_img, dtype=np.float32)

    # Change HWC to CHW
    img = img.swapaxes(1, 2).swapaxes(0, 1)

    # Change RGB to BGR
    img = img[(2, 1, 0), :, :]

    # Mean subtraction
    img = img - MEAN

    # Change CHW to NCHW by adding batch dimension at front
    img = img[np.newaxis, :, :, :]

    return img
```

In the preceding code, we first used the `PIL.Image` module to read in the image from the input file as a 3-channel byte values. We then resized the image to the size required by AlexNet and used NumPy, which made the rest of the image processing easier. PIL reads the image channels in the order `HWC` (height, width, channel) and the channels are in `RGB` order. But AlexNet expects the data to be laid out as `BGR` channels of `HW` size. So, we converted to that format. Finally, we subtracted the mean from the image values and then added in a batch dimension in front to reformat the data to `NCHW` format.

Loading the ONNX model from a file is easy if you use the `load` method from the `onnx` package, as follows:

```
model = onnx.load("alexnet.onnx")
```

Finally, we can use the loaded ONNX model for inference directly, using the `predict_img_class` method described as follows:

```
def predict_img_class(onnx_model, img):
    """Get image class determined by network."""

    results = caffe2.python.onnx.backend.run_model(onnx_model, [img])
    class_index = np.argmax(results[0])
    class_prob = results[0][0, class_index]

    imgnet_classes = json.load(open("imagenet1000.json"))
    class_name = imgnet_classes[class_index]

    return class_index, class_name, class_prob
```

We need to use the `run_model` method, provided by Caffe2 ONNX backend `caffe2.python.backend`, to pass the inputs and obtain the results after inference through this model. Because we used an ImageNet model, we should use a JSON file with the mapping from the ImageNet class index number to its class name. We should pick the class index with the highest probability value and find its ImageNet class name.

Visualizing the ONNX model

When working with ONNX models, it can be useful to have a tool that can help in visualizing the network structure. ONNX ships with such a script called `net_drawer.py`. You can find this tool in the `onnx/onnx/tools` directory in the ONNX source repository. If you installed ONNX from its Python package, then you can find this script at `/usr/local/lib/python2.7/dist-packages/onnx/tools/net_drawer.py`.

This script can be applied to convert an ONNX file to a directed acyclic graph representation of the network in the GraphViz DOT format. For example, consider the ONNX file `alexnet.onnx` that we obtained in the earlier section on converting from the Caffe2 model to the ONNX model.

We can convert this AlexNet ONNX file to a DOT file using the following command:

```
$ python /usr/local/lib/python2.7/dist-packages/onnx/tools/net_drawer.py --
input alexnet.onnx --output alexnet.dot
```

To convert the DOT file to a PNG image file for viewing, use the following command:

```
$ dot alexnet.dot -Tpng -o alexnet.png
```

The image thus produced, shows the visualization of AlexNet

Another excellent visualization tool for ONNX models is Netron. The usage of this tool is covered in `Chapter 7`, *Caffe2 at the Edge and in the cloud.*

Summary

In this chapter, we introduced the details of the ONNX format, a popular representation for DL models. We examined how it depicts the intermediate representation and operators. We then looked at support for ONNX in Caffe2. Using AlexNet as the example, we looked at how to convert a Caffe2 model file to ONNX format. We also looked at the reverse process: importing an ONNX model file into Caffe2, and then using it for inference. Finally, we looked at a useful tool to visualize the graph representation of an ONNX file.

6
Deploying Models to Accelerators for Inference

In Chapter 3, *Training Networks*, we learned how to train deep neural networks using Caffe2. In this chapter, we will focus on inference: deploying a trained model in the field to *infer* results on new data. For efficient inference, the trained model is typically optimized for the accelerator on which it is deployed. In this chapter, we will focus on two popular accelerators: GPUs and CPUs, and the inference engines TensorRT and OpenVINO, which can be used to deploy Caffe2 models on them.

In this chapter, we will look at the following topics:

- Inference engines
- NVIDIA TensorRT
- Intel OpenVINO

Inference engines

Popular DL frameworks, such as TensorFlow, PyTorch, and Caffe, are designed primarily for *training* deep neural networks. They focus on offering features that are more useful for researchers to experiment easily with different types of network structures, training regimens, and techniques to achieve optimum training accuracy to solve a particular problem in the real world. After a neural network model has been successfully trained, practitioners could continue to use the same DL framework for deploying the trained model for inference. However, there are more efficient deployment solutions for inference. These are pieces of inference software that compile a trained model into a computation engine that is most efficient in latency or throughput on the accelerator hardware used for deployment.

Much like a C or C++ compiler, inference engines take the trained model as input and apply several optimization techniques on the graph structure, layers, weights, and formats of the trained neural network. For example, they might remove layers that are only useful in training. The engine might fuse multiple horizontally adjacent layers, or vertically adjacent layers, together for faster computation and a lower number of memory accesses.

While training is typically performed in FP32 (4 bytes floating point), inference engines might offer inference in lower-precision data types such as FP16 (2 bytes floating point) and INT8 (1 byte integer). To achieve this, these engines might convert the weight parameters of the model to lower precision and might use quantization. Using these lower-precision data types typically speeds up inference by a large factor, while degrading the accuracy of your trained networks by a negligible amount.

The inference engines and libraries available right now typically focus on optimizing the trained model for a particular type of accelerator hardware. For example, the NVIDIA TensorRT inference engine (not to be confused with the Google TensorFlow DL framework) focuses on optimizing your trained neural network for inference on NVIDIA graphics cards and embedded devices. Similarly, the Intel OpenVINO inference engine focuses on optimizing trained networks for Intel CPUs and accelerators.

In the rest of the chapter, we will look at how to deploy Caffe2 models for inference on GPUs and CPUs, by using TensorRT and OpenVINO as the inference engines.

NVIDIA TensorRT

TensorRT is the most popular inference engine for deploying trained models on NVIDIA GPUs for inference. Not surprisingly, this library and its set of tools are developed by NVIDIA and it is available free for download and use. A new version of TensorRT typically accompanies the release of every new NVIDIA GPU architecture, adding optimizations for the new GPU architecture and also support for new types of layers, operators, and DL frameworks.

Installing TensorRT

TensorRT installers can be downloaded from the web at `https://developer.nvidia.com/tensorrt`. Installation packages are available for x86-64 (Intel or AMD 64-bit CPU) computers, PowerPC computers, embedded hardware such as NVIDIA TX1/TX2, and NVIDIA Xavier systems used in automobiles. Operating systems supported include Linux, Windows, and QNX (a realtime OS used in automobiles).

For Linux, multiple LTS versions of Ubuntu are supported, for example, 14.04, 16.04, and 18.04. Other Linux distributions, such as CentOS/Red Hat are also supported. Every TensorRT package is built for a particular version of CUDA, such as 9.0 or 10.0, for example. A typical installer's download web page is shown in Figure 6.1, as follows:

TensorRT 5.0 GA for Linux

Documentation

- Support Matrix Guide
- Installation Guide
- Release Notes
- Developer Guide

Debian and RPM Install Packages

- TensorRT 5.0.2.6 GA for Ubuntu 1804 and CUDA 10.0 DEB local repo packages
- TensorRT 5.0.2.6 GA for Ubuntu 1604 and CUDA 10.0 DEB local repo packages
- TensorRT 5.0.2.6 GA for Ubuntu 1604 and CUDA 9.0 DEB local repo packages
- TensorRT 5.0.2.6 GA for Ubuntu 1404 and CUDA 10.0 DEB local repo packages
- TensorRT 5.0.2.6 GA for Ubuntu 1404 and CUDA 9.0 DEB local repo packages
- TensorRT 5.0.2.6 GA for CentOS/RedHat 7 and CUDA 10.0 RPM local repo packages
- TensorRT 5.0.2.6 GA for CentOS/RedHat 7 and CUDA 9.0 RPM local repo packages

Tar File Install Packages

- TensorRT 5.0.2.6 GA for Ubuntu 18.04 and CUDA 10.0 tar package
- TensorRT 5.0.2.6 GA for Ubuntu 16.04 and CUDA 10.0 tar package
- TensorRT 5.0.2.6 GA for Ubuntu 16.04 and CUDA 9.0 tar package
- TensorRT 5.0.2.6 GA for Ubuntu 14.04 and CUDA 10.0 tar package
- TensorRT 5.0.2.6 GA for Ubuntu 14.04 and CUDA 9.0 tar package
- TensorRT 5.0.2.6 GA for CentOS/RedHat 7 and CUDA 10.0 tar package
- TensorRT 5.0.2.6 GA for CentOS/RedHat 7 and CUDA 9.0 tar package

TensorRT 5.0 GA For Windows

Documentation

- Installation Guide
- Release Notes
- Developer Guide
- Support Matrix
- Best Practices

Windows ZIP Package

- Windows10 and CUDA 10.0 zip package
- Windows10 and CUDA 9.0 zip package

TensorRT is also available on the following NVIDIA GPU platforms:

- NVIDIA GPU Cloud (NGC) TensorRT Container for cloud deployment
- NVIDIA Jetpack for Jetson embedded platforms
- NVIDIA DriveInstall for NVIDIA DRIVE autonomous driving platform (access requires membership of the NVIDIA Drive Developer Program)

Figure 6.1: Installer's web page for TensorRT version 5.0. Notice the Installation Guide, packages for Ubuntu, Red Hat, Windows, and also Jetpack for embedded systems and DRIVE for automobiles

You will need to download the TensorRT installer that matches your hardware, operating system, and installed CUDA version. For example, on my x86-64 notebook running Ubuntu 18.04, I have CUDA 10.0 installed. So, I will download the installer that matches this setup.

Once you have downloaded the installer package, follow the instructions provided in the **TensorRT Installation Guide** document to install it. You can find this guide as a PDF document on the installer page (see Figure 6.1). Installing typically entails using `sudo dpkg -i` for a package on Ubuntu, or using `yum` on Red Hat. If you downloaded a `.tar.gz` archive, then you can extract it to a location of your choice. No matter how you install it, the TensorRT package includes these components: C++ header files, C++ shared library files, C++ samples, Python library, and Python samples.

Using TensorRT

Using TensorRT for inference typically involves the following three stages:

1. Importing a pre-trained network or creating a network
2. Building an optimized engine from the network
3. Inference using execution context of an engine

We will examine these three stages in detail in the following sections.

Importing a pre-trained network or creating a network

Models are trained in DL frameworks, such as Caffe2, Caffe, PyTorch, or TensorFlow. Some practitioners might use their own custom frameworks to train models. The first step is to build a network structure inside TensorRT and load the pre-trained weights from these DL framework models into the layers of the TensorRT network. This process is described in Figure 6.2, as follows:

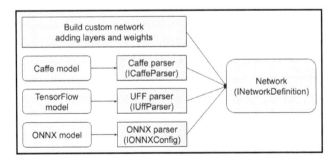

Figure 6.2: How a network can be built in TensorRT

If you trained a model using popular DL frameworks, then TensorRT provides **parsers** to parse your pre-trained model files and build a network from it. TensorRT provides an ONNX parser named `IONNXConfig` that can be used to load and import your Caffe2 pre-trained model file that has been converted to ONNX. You can find information on how to convert a Caffe2 model to ONNX in `Chapter 5`, *Working with Other Frameworks*.

TensorRT provides a Caffe parser named `ICaffeParser` that can be used to load and import your Caffe model. Similarly, it also provides a TensorFlow parser named `IUffConfig` to load and import your TensorFlow model.

Not all layers and operators from Caffe2, ONNX, or other frameworks might be supported in TensorRT. Also, if you trained a model using your own custom training framework then you cannot use these parsers. To cover such scenarios, TensorRT provides users with the ability to create a network layer by layer. Custom layers that are not supported in TensorRT can be implemented using TensorRT plugins. You would typically need to implement an unsupported layer in CUDA for optimum performance with TensorRT. Examples of all these use cases are depicted in the samples that ship with TensorRT.

No matter which of the preceding processes you follow, you end up with a TensorRT network called `INetworkDefinition`. This can be used in the second stage for optimization.

Building an optimized engine from the network

Once a network and its weights are represented inside TensorRT, we can then optimize this network definition. This optimization step is performed by a module called the **builder**. The builder should be executed on the same GPU on which you plan to perform inference later. Though models are trained using FP32 precision, you can request the builder to use lower-precision FP16 or INT8 data types that occupy less memory and might have optimized instructions on certain GPUs. This is shown in Figure 6.3, as follows:

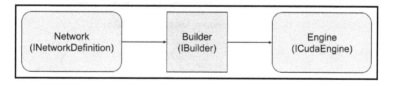

Figure 6.3: Build process in TensorRT to produce an engine

The builder tries various optimizations specific to the GPU that you run it on. It tries kernels and data formats that are specific to the GPU architecture and GPU model that you run it on. It times all of these optimization opportunities and picks the optimal candidates. This optimized version of the network that it produces is called an **engine**. This engine can be serialized to a file commonly known as the **PLAN file**.

Inference using execution context of an engine

To use an engine for inference in TensorRT, we first need to create a runtime. The runtime can be used to load an engine from a PLAN file after deserializing it. We can then create one or more execution contexts from the runtime and use those for runtime inference. This process is depicted in Figure 6.4, as follows:

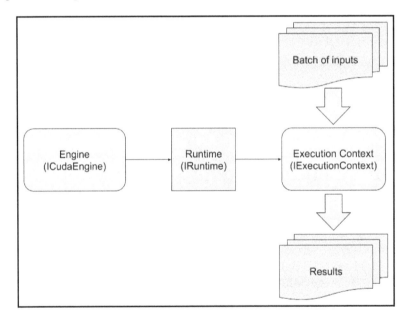

Figure 6.4: Process of inference using an engine in TensorRT

TensorRT API and usage

TensorRT provides both a C++ API and a Python API for your use. These APIs can be used to perform all the three stages depicted in the earlier sections. You can look at the samples that are provided along with TensorRT to understand how to write your own C++ and Python programs that do this. For example, the sampleMNISTAPI sample that ships with TensorRT shows how to build a simple network to solve the MNIST problem (introduced in Chapter 2, *Composing Networks*) and load pre-trained weights into each of the layers.

To use the C++ API, you would essentially include the NvInfer.h, and related header files, and compile your program. When you need to link your program, you would need to make sure that the libnvinfer.so and other related TensorRT library files are in your LD_LIBRARY_PATH environment variable.

TensorRT ships with a tool named trtexec that can be used to experiment with an import of a pre-trained model and use it for inference. As an example, we will illustrate how to use our AlexNet ONNX model from Chapter 5, *Working with Other Frameworks*, for inference in TensorRT.

First, we need to import our AlexNet ONNX model file (converted from Caffe2 protobuf file) and build an optimized engine file from it. This can be done using trtexec, as follows:

```
./trtexec --onnx=/path/to/alexnet.onnx --output=prob --
saveEngine=alexnet.plan
```

The --onnx option is used to point to the input ONNX file. There are similar --deploy and --uff options available if you are importing Caffe or TensorFlow models, respectively. The --output option is used to specify the name of the final output from the model. There is a similar --input option to point out an input to the model. Multiple instances of the --input and --output options can be used if the model has multiple inputs or outputs. The --saveEngine option is used to indicate a file path that the tool will use to serialize the optimized engine to. For more information, please try ./trtexec --help.

Next, we can load the saved optimized engine and then use it for inference, as follows:

```
./trtexec --output=prob --loadEngine=alexnet.plan
```

The tool deserializes the PLAN file to an engine, creates a runtime from the engine and then creates an execution context from the runtime. It uses this context to run batches of random inputs and reports the inference runtime performance of this model on the GPU you ran it on. The source code of `trtexec` and all TensorRT samples is available in the TensorRT package. This source code is a good instructional aid to learning how to incorporate TensorRT into your inference application in C++ or Python.

Intel OpenVINO

OpenVINO consists of libraries and tools created by Intel that enable you to optimize your trained DL model from any framework and then deploy it using an inference engine on Intel hardware. Supported hardware includes Intel CPUs, integrated graphics in Intel CPUs, Intel's Movidius Neural Compute Stick, and FPGAs. OpenVINO is available for free from Intel.

OpenVINO includes the following components:

- **Model optimizer**: A tool that imports trained DL models from other DL frameworks, converts them, and then optimizes them. Supported DL frameworks include Caffe, TensorFlow, MXNet, and ONNX. Note the absence of support for Caffe2 or PyTorch.
- **Inference engine**: These are libraries that load the optimized model produced by the model optimizer and provide your applications with the ability to run the model on Intel hardware.
- **Demos and samples**: These simple applications demonstrate the use of OpenVINO and help you integrate it into your application.

 OpenVINO is meant for inference; it provides no features to research new network structures or train neural networks. Using OpenVINO is a big topic by itself. In this book, we will focus on how to install it, test it, and use Caffe2 models with it for inference.

Installing OpenVINO

In this section, we will look at the steps to install and test OpenVINO on Ubuntu. The steps to install and test on other Linux distributions, such as CentOS, and other operating systems, such as Windows, is similar. For guidance on all of these, please refer to the *OpenVINO Installation Guide* suitable for your operating system. It is available online and in the installer.

Installation files of OpenVINO for your operating system or Linux distribution can be downloaded from `https://software.intel.com/en-us/openvino-toolkit`. For example, for Ubuntu it gives me the option of downloading a **Customizable Package** or a single large **Full Package**. Figure 6.5 shows these options, as follows:

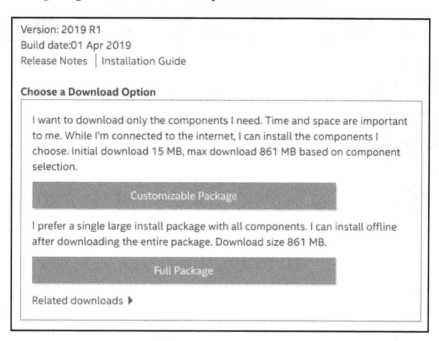

Figure 6.5: OpenVINO installer options for download on Ubuntu

The downloaded file typically has a filename of the form `l_openvino_toolkit_p_<version>.tgz`. Uncompress the contents of this file to a directory and change to that directory. Here you will find installer shell scripts available in two formats: console or GUI. Either of these can be executed as follows:

```
$ sudo ./install_GUI.sh
$ sudo ./install.sh
```

Both of these options provide a helpful wizard to enable you to choose where you want to install OpenVINO files and what components of OpenVINO you would like to install. If you run the scripts without `sudo`, they will provide you with an option to install to an `intel` subdirectory inside your home directory. Running with `sudo` helps you install to `/opt/intel`, which is where most Intel tools traditionally get installed.

Figure 6.6 shows the OpenVINO components that can be chosen during installation. At a minimum, I recommend installing the **Model Optimizer**, **Inference Engine**, and **OpenCV**. OpenCV will be needed if you want to read images and feed them to the inference engine. Figure 6.6 is as follows:

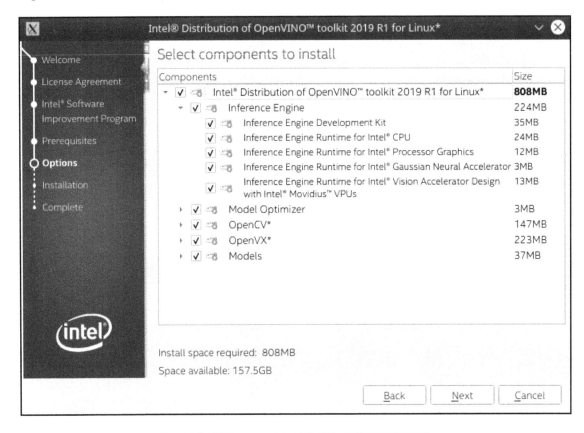

Figure 6.6: OpenVINO components that can be installed using the GUI installer wizard

After the main installation, we also need to install some external dependencies of OpenVINO by completing the following these commands:

```
$ cd /opt/intel/openvino/install_dependencies
$ chmod +x install_openvino_dependencies.sh
$ sudo -E ./install_openvino_dependencies.sh
```

If you did not install using sudo, you can replace /opt/intel in the preceding command with the path where you installed OpenVINO in your home directory.

Now we are ready to set up the environment variables needed for OpenVINO. We can do this by using the following command:

```
$ source /opt/intel/openvino/bin/setupvars.sh
```

We next configure OpenVINO to support the DL frameworks whose models we want to import. We can pull in the configurations for all supported DL frameworks by using the following command:

```
$ cd
/opt/intel/openvino/deployment_tools/model_optimizer/install_prerequisites
$ sudo ./install_prerequisites.sh
```

We are now ready to test if our OpenVINO installation is working. We can do this by running an OpenVINO demo that downloads a *SqueezeNet* model trained using Caffe, optimizes it using the Model Optimizer, and runs it using the Inference Engine on an image of a car, as follows:

```
$ cd /opt/intel/openvino/deployment_tools/demo
$ ./demo_squeezenet_download_convert_run.sh
```

On running this, we should be able to see a classification result for the car image. The class with the highest probability score is a sports car, thus confirming that the model inference using OpenVINO is working. This is shown in Figure 6.7, as follows:

```
Top 10 results:

Image /home/ashwin/intel/openvino_2019.1.094/deployment_tools/demo/car.png

classid probability label
------- ----------- -----
817     0.8363345   sports car, sport car
511     0.0946488   convertible
479     0.0419131   car wheel
751     0.0091071   racer, race car, racing car
436     0.0068161   beach wagon, station wagon, wagon, estate car, beach waggon, station waggon, waggon
656     0.0037564   minivan
586     0.0025741   half track
717     0.0016069   pickup, pickup truck
864     0.0012027   tow truck, tow car, wrecker
581     0.0005882   grille, radiator grille


total inference time: 5.8661839
Average running time of one iteration: 5.8661839 ms

Throughput: 170.4685733 FPS
```

Figure 6.7: OpenVINO demo classification results on a sports car image

Model conversion

OpenVINO does not support the Caffe2 model format. However, it does support the popular ONNX representation for models. So, to use a Caffe2 model with OpenVINO we should follow a two-step process.

First, we need to convert our Caffe2 model to the ONNX format. This process is described in detail in Chapter 5, *Working with Other Frameworks*. After that, we can use the ONNX model thus produced with the OpenVINO Model Optimizer to import, optimize and convert it to the OpenVINO **Intermediate Representation (IR)** format.

Let's examine this Model Optimizer process with the AlexNet model that we converted to ONNX in Chapter 5, *Working with Other Frameworks*. We had converted the AlexNet Caffe2 model to produce an alexnet.onnx file.

To convert this AlexNet ONNX model to the OpenVINO IR using Model Optimizer, we can use the mo.py script as follows:

```
$ cd /opt/intel/openvino/deployment_tools/model_optimizer
$ python3 mo.py --input_model /path/to/alexnet.onnx
Model Optimizer arguments:
Common parameters:
        - Path to the Input Model:      /path/to/alexnet.onnx
        - Path for generated IR:
/opt/intel/openvino_2019.1.094/deployment_tools/model_optimizer/.
        - IR output name:       alexnet
        - Log level:    ERROR
        - Batch:        Not specified, inherited from the model
        - Input layers:         Not specified, inherited from the model
        - Output layers:        Not specified, inherited from the model
        - Input shapes:         Not specified, inherited from the model
        - Mean values:          Not specified
        - Scale values:         Not specified
        - Scale factor:         Not specified
        - Precision of IR:      FP32
        - Enable fusing:        True
        - Enable grouped convolutions fusing:   True
        - Move mean values to preprocess section:       False
        - Reverse input channels:       False
ONNX specific parameters:
Model Optimizer version:        2019.1.0-341-gc9b66a2

[ SUCCESS ] Generated IR model.
[ SUCCESS ] XML file:
/opt/intel/openvino_2019.1.094/deployment_tools/model_optimizer/./alexnet.x
ml
```

```
[ SUCCESS ] BIN file:
/opt/intel/openvino_2019.1.094/deployment_tools/model_optimizer/./alexnet.b
in
[ SUCCESS ] Total execution time: 6.48 seconds.
```

This conversion process produces three files:

- `.bin` file: This file contains the weights of the model. This is the reason why this is typically a large file.
- `.xml` file: This is an XML file containing the network structure. Details stored inside this file include metadata about the model, the list of layers, configuration parameters of each layer, and the list of edges between the layers.
- `.mapping` file: This is an XML file that has the mapping from the input file layers to the output OpenVINO file layers.

We only need the `.bin` file and the `.xml` file to use the model with the OpenVINO Inference Engine.

Model inference

OpenVINO provides an Inference Engine API in both C++ and Python. This API can be used to create network structures programmatically for your trained Caffe2 models. You can then load the weights of each network layer into the OpenVINO network and use that for inference on Intel hardware. If OpenVINO does not currently support the type of network layer or operator that your trained model is using, then you will need to implement that using a plugin layer in OpenVINO. All this effort is worth it because you will benefit from gains in latency and throughput for your Caffe2 trained models once they are running using the OpenVINO Inference Engine.

For most networks, there is an easier alternative: convert your Caffe2 trained model to OpenVINO IR using the OpenVINO Model Optimizer. We looked at how to do this in the previous section. After this step, use the features in OpenVINO Inference Engine to import this IR model automatically for inference. OpenVINO provides many Inference Engine samples that can be used to try this process out.

Remember to run the `/opt/intel/openvino/bin/setupvars.sh` script before you do this. This script sets up the necessary environment variables and settings for OpenVINO use.

Go to the Inference Engine `samples` directory and examine the various samples. There are samples to suit many common use cases. For example, there are samples to test classification models, to test object detection models, to test text detection, to test the latency and throughput performance, and more.

To build all the Inference Engine samples, follow these steps:

```
$ cd /opt/intel/openvino/deployment_tools/inference_engine/samples
$ ./build_samples.sh
```

The Inference Engine samples will be built using CMake. The sample binary files are installed into a directory called `inference_engine_samples_build/intel64/Release` under your home directory.

These samples make it very convenient to quickly try the OpenVINO Inference Engine on an IR model. These samples may use some extra libraries that are installed along with OpenVINO. So, if you find that a sample needs a library (`.so` file) that is missing, you may need to add the path to that library to the `LD_LIBRARY_PATH` environment variable.

I found that using the following `LD_LIBRARY_PATH` worked for me:

```
$ export
LD_LIBRARY_PATH=/opt/intel/openvino/deployment_tools/inference_engine/exter
nal/mkltiny_lnx/lib:/opt/intel/openvino/deployment_tools/inference_engine/l
ib:.:$LD_LIBRARY_PATH
```

One of the simplest samples to try is `hello_classification`. This sample takes two inputs: a path to an OpenVINO IR classification model and a path to an image file. It creates an OpenVINO Inference Engine by importing the IR model and running inference on it using the image.

To try the OpenVINO Inference Engine on the IR model we created earlier from our AlexNet Caffe2 model, use the following command:

```
$ ./hello_classification /path/to/alexnet.xml /path/to/sunflower.jpg

Top 10 results:
Image /path/to/sunflower.jpg
classid probability
------- -----------
985     0.9568181
309     0.0330606
328     0.0035365
946     0.0012036
308     0.0007907
310     0.0005121
```

```
723      0.0004805
108      0.0004062
950      0.0003640
947      0.0003286
```

We can see that the `hello_classification` sample successfully loaded the IR model into its inference engine and ran classification on the input sunflower image. It reported the ImageNet class 985 (daisy) as the highest score, which is the closest matching class for sunflower among the 1,000 ImageNet classes.

OpenVINO Inference Engine can be used to perform inference in FP16 and also INT8 modes. Please refer to the OpenVINO documentation for details.

Summary

In this chapter, we learned about inference engines and how they are an essential tool for the final deployment of a trained Caffe2 model on accelerators. We focused on two types of popular accelerators: NVIDIA GPUs and Intel CPUs. We looked at how to install and use TensorRT for deploying our Caffe2 model on NVIDIA GPUs. We also looked at the installation and use of OpenVINO for deploying our Caffe2 model on Intel CPUs and accelerators.

Many other companies, such as Google, Facebook, Amazon, and start-ups such as Habana and GraphCore, are developing new accelerator hardware for the inference of DL models. There are also efforts such as ONNX Runtime that are bringing together the inference engines from multiple vendors under one umbrella. Please evaluate these options and choose which accelerator hardware and software works best for deployment of your Caffe2 model.

In the next chapter, we will take a look at Caffe2 at the edge on Raspberry Pi, Caffe2 in the cloud using containers, and Caffe2 model visualization.

7
Caffe2 at the Edge and in the cloud

In chapters 1-6 of this book, we have learned how to install and use Caffe2 to train DL neural networks and how to work with other popular DL frameworks. We have also learnt how to deploy our trained Caffe2 models on popular inference engines. In this last chapter, we will look at applications of Caffe2 that exploit its ability to scale from tiny edge devices such as the Raspberry Pi to running on containers in the cloud. We will also look at visualizing Caffe2 models.

The topics that will be covered in this chapter are as follows:

- Caffe2 at the edge on Raspberry Pi
- Caffe2 in the cloud using containers
- Caffe2 model visualization

Caffe2 at the edge on Raspberry Pi

There is a lot of interest in using deep learning at the edge. This is the application of deep learning to compute solutions on or near the devices that capture data using sensors and cameras. An alternative solution to deep learning at the edge is to capture edge data and send it to in the cloud for processing. But, deep learning at the edge has the advantage of lower latency and higher security. Devices at the edge are typically cheap, have a small form factor and use less power, and their processors or accelerators have less compute capability. One of the key advantages of Caffe2 is that it has been designed and developed from the beginning to scale: from multi-GPU, multi-CPU servers, down to tiny edge devices. In this section, we will use the Raspberry Pi as an example of an edge device and learn how to use Caffe2 on it.

Raspberry Pi

The Raspberry Pi is a series of single-board general-purpose computers introduced by the Raspberry Pi Foundation from the UK. *Figure 7.1* shows the latest Rv3 board of the Raspberry Pi B+ unit, as follows:

Figure 7.1: A Raspberry Pi B+ Rev3 board, released in 2018

Since its introduction in 2012, the Pi has taken the world by storm, being used for teaching in schools, for hobby projects, and real-world deployments at the edge. Costing about $35 each, the Pi is affordable for all types of projects. What makes the Raspberry Pi computer so useful is its small form factor; it is about the size of a pack of cards. The Pi requires little power, running off a 5V micro-USB power supply. And the Pi is a fully general-purpose computer, with all common storage and I/O ports, such as SD/microSD card slots, USB ports, wireless connectivity, an Ethernet port, an HDMI out, and a composite video out. Probably the biggest advantage of the Pi over other devices in its form factor is the availability of Raspbian, a port of the popular Debian Linux distribution for the Pi. With Raspbian, Pi users get to use the same tools, compilers and programming libraries that are available on a mainstream Linux distribution.

Our Caffe2 experiment on the Raspberry Pi will involve the following steps:

1. Installing Raspbian
2. Building and using Caffe2 on Raspbian

Installing Raspbian

Follow these steps to install Raspbian:

1. Download Raspbian releases from `https://www.raspberrypi.org/downloads/raspbian/`. There is a Raspbian release corresponding to every Debian release. The latest Debian version 9 is called **Stretch** and the corresponding Raspbian is called Raspbian 9 or Raspbian Stretch.
2. Choose a Raspbian bundle that is appropriate for you. To suit various applications, there are three type of Raspbian Stretch bundles that are available. For our purpose, the smallest bundle called **Raspbian Stretch Lite** is adequate. If you would like to use a desktop and GUI apps, then you can try the other bundles that ship with those features. Once your Raspbian is connected to your network, you can SSH into it and get full access to a Bash shell to run commands and console tools and editors. You could also choose to install other GUI applications later if you required them. Stretch Lite is sufficient for all these purposes.
3. Pick a tool to flash the Raspbian disk image to an SD card. A recommended easy-to-use tool for this purpose is **Etcher**. Download it from `https://www.balena.io/etcher/`.
4. Once you have installed Etcher, plug in an SD card with a minimum of 4 GB capacity into your computer's SD card slot. Use Etcher to flash the Raspbian disk image to the SD card.

 The Raspberry Pi can be used as a headless computer by SSHing to it instead of working at it locally. If you would like this feature to be enabled from the very first boot up of Raspbian then put back the flashed SD card into your computer. Then, create an empty file named `ssh` in the root directory of the SD card.

5. Now we are done with flashing the SD card with Raspbian. Insert this SD card into the SD card slot on the Raspberry Pi board. Make sure your Pi is connected to your home wireless router with an Ethernet cable. Optionally, you can also connect your Pi to your TV or computer display with an HDMI cable to watch its boot messages.

6. Power on the Pi. You can see the boot messages of Raspbian on your TV or display. At the end of the boot-up sequence, it displays the IP address assigned to it by DHCP and asks you to log in locally. Alternatively, you can also figure out the IP address allocated to the Pi by checking the admin console of your wireless router. Now you can SSH into the Raspbian from any computer on the network using the following command:

```
$ ssh pi@<IP address of Pi>
```

7. Use the default password: `raspberry`. After your first successful login, Raspbian will remind you to change the default password. Please do so by typing the `passwd` command at the shell. You can use this new password from the next time you SSH into the Pi.

8. Finally, make sure to update the package repositories and update the installed packages using the following commands:

```
$ sudo apt update
$ sudo apt upgrade
```

Building Caffe2 on Raspbian

Caffe2 has been ported to Raspbian. But there is no easy way to cross-compile to the Raspberry Pi from your x86_64 computer, so Caffe2 has to be built on the diminutive Pi itself.

We could SSH to the Pi and clone the Caffe2 Git repository on it. However, the full PyTorch and Caffe2 repository, along with their submodules, is more than 400 MB, and that clone operation could take a long time to complete on the Pi. Also, note that it is fastest to clone to the SD card rather than a hard disk connected by USB to the Pi. The latter can be painfully slow because Pi only has USB 2.0 (which is slower than USB 3.0) and the USB ports and Ethernet ports share the same bus, further limiting the Git clone speed.

Let's get started with building Caffe 2 on Raspbian:

1. Since it is easiest to clone on your local computer, let's do that first using the following commands:

```
$ git clone --recursive https://github.com/pytorch/pytorch.git
$ cd pytorch
$ git submodule update --init
```

2. Once the clone is done, reduce the size of this directory by deleting the Git repository data, as follows:

```
$ rm -rf .git
```

3. Now compress this into a `.tar.gz` archive and copy it over SSH to the Pi, as follows:

```
$ cd ..
$ tar zcvf pytorch.tar.gz pytorch
$ scp pytorch.tar.gz pi@<IP address of Pi>:/home/pi
```

4. SSH to the Pi and decompress the copied archive there, as follows:

```
$ tar xvf pytorch.tar.gz
$ cd pytorch
```

5. The script to build Caffe2 on Raspbian is `scripts/build_raspbian.sh`. Note that this Raspbian build has not been maintained in recent times. So, before we run it, we need to install a few Python packages that are necessary for successful compilation, as follows:

```
$ sudo apt install python-future python-typing python-yaml
$ sudo pip install -U protobuf
```

6. We are now ready to build by invoking the following script:

```
$ cd scripts
$ ./build_raspbian.sh
```

7. Just like the build process we used in Chapter 1, *Introduction and Installation*, this also uses CMake, first to configure the make process and then to invoke make to build the necessary components, placing the built artifacts in the build subdirectory.

Note that the build process takes a long time and could take as much as half a day. The Raspberry Pi has 500 MB to 1 GB of RAM (depending on which variant of Pi you have) and Raspbian, by default, allocates only about 100 MB of swap space. So, the build can fail sometimes because it runs out of memory. If that happens, you can increase the swap space by opening the `/etc/dphys-swapfile` file and increasing the `CONF_SWAPSIZE` value. I found that increasing it from `100` to `1000` was sufficient for successful compilation.

After compilation, you can install and test Caffe2 just as we did in `Chapter 1`, *Introduction and Installation*, as shown in the following example:

```
$ cd ../build
$ sudo make install
$ python -c "from caffe2.python import core"
```

You now have Caffe2 working on the Raspberry Pi. You can now attach sensors or camera modules to the Pi, read images and data from them, and run them through DL networks for classification, detection, and understanding.

Caffe2 in the cloud using containers

Containers are now a ubiquitous and necessary tool for robustly deploying software in production, both locally and in the cloud. They enable developers to create the ideal software environment for the application and ensure that this software environment is exactly replicated on developer workstations, test computers, staging computers, and the final deployment to local servers or instances in the cloud. Containers also help create a sanitized software environment for every single application, enabling multiple software environments, one for each application, when multiple applications are running on the same server.

Among the many available container tools, *Docker* is the most popular. We will focus on using Docker in this section. Docker is available for all popular Linux distributions, macOS X, and Windows. With Docker, you can create an Ubuntu software environment from a specific Ubuntu version and run your Caffe2 application inside that on a RedHat host OS from a different version. Docker makes such varied deployments easy and doable in mere minutes.

Installing Docker

Follow these steps for installation:

1. To install Docker using package repositories and packages specific to your OS or distribution, please follow the instructions here `https://docs.docker.com/engine/installation/linux/docker-ce/ubuntu/`.

2. After the installation is successful, remember to add your username to the `docker` user group using a command like the one shown in the following example:

   ```
   $ sudo adduser myusername docker
   ```

   For this addition to the group to take full effect, you may need to log out and log back in again.

3. And, finally, to test if your Docker setup is working correctly, run the `hello-world` image. If successful, you will see a welcoming message similar to the following example:

   ```
   $ docker run hello-world

   Hello from Docker!
   This message shows that your installation appears to be working
   correctly.

   To generate this message, Docker took the following steps:
    1. The Docker client contacted the Docker daemon.
    2. The Docker daemon pulled the "hello-world" image from the
   Docker Hub.
       (amd64)
    3. The Docker daemon created a new container from that image which
       runs the executable that produces the output you are currently
       reading.
    4. The Docker daemon streamed that output to the Docker client,
       which sent it to your terminal.

   To try something more ambitious, you can run an Ubuntu container
   with:
    $ docker run -it ubuntu bash

   Share images, automate workflows, and more with a free Docker ID:
    https://hub.docker.com/

   For more examples and ideas, visit:
    https://docs.docker.com/get-started/
   ```

As a final experiment, you can get a Bash shell inside an Ubuntu container and explore inside that Ubuntu instance by using the following command:

```
$ docker run --rm -it ubuntu bash
```

Here we are launching an Ubuntu container. The -it option indicates that this is an interactive session. That is, we want to run the application (bash) and stay with it until we quit the container. This is opposed to the normal flow (such as in the hello-world container) where Docker executes an application and quits once it is completed. The --rm option indicates that Docker should tear down the container once we quit it. Normally, it would keep it around in the background, ready for use again.

You will notice that Docker logs you in as the root user and you get a root shell. You are placed at the root of the filesystem. The root privileges are only inside this Docker container. Any files you create or change inside the container are ephemeral. They are lost when you exit the container.

Once you are done exploring the Ubuntu container, you can quit by pressing *Ctrl + D* or typing exit.

Installing nvidia-docker

You can run Caffe2, Python, and C++ applications on the CPU in Docker after following the preceding steps. However, if you want to run Caffe2 applications on the GPU, then you need to install and use nvidia-docker.

NVIDIA-Docker provides full and unfettered access to the NVIDIA GPUs on your system to your applications running inside Docker. Note that this feature relies on the NVIDIA GPU driver installed on your host system. However, you do not need to install CUDA or cuDNN on your host system because you can spin up a container having any CUDA version you want installed inside it. This is a convenient way to build and test your applications against different CUDA versions.

The instructions for installing NVIDIA Docker can be found at https://github.com/NVIDIA/nvidia-docker. At the time of writing, nvidia-docker could be installed using the following steps:

1. First, add the nvidia-docker repositories and update the package cache, as follows:

```
$ curl -s -L https://nvidia.github.io/nvidia-docker/gpgkey | sudo
apt-key add - distribution=$(. /etc/os-release;echo $ID$VERSION_ID)
$ curl -s -L
```

```
https://nvidia.github.io/nvidia-docker/$distribution/nvidia-docker.
list | sudo tee /etc/apt/sources.list.d/nvidia-docker.list
$ sudo apt-get update
```

2. Next, install the NVIDIA Docker runtime, as follows:

```
$ sudo apt-get install -y nvidia-docker2
```

3. And, finally, restart the Docker daemon, as follows:

```
$ sudo pkill -SIGHUP dockerd
```

We are now ready to test if our NVIDIA Docker is working and can access the NVIDIA GPU on our system. To do this we need to run the application `nvidia-smi` in the container, as follows:

```
$ docker run --runtime=nvidia --rm nvidia/cuda:9.0-base nvidia-smi
```

`nvidia-smi` is a tool that talks to the NVIDIA GPU driver on your host system to print information about the GPUs available on your system. If your NVIDIA Docker installation is successful, you should be able to see the `nvidia-smi` list, the NVIDIA GPU driver version and the GPUs you have installed on it.

Note the Docker tag we used in this command: `nvidia/cuda:9.0-base`. This is a Docker image that has CUDA 9.0 installed inside it. The full list of available Docker images and tags can be seen here: `https://hub.docker.com/r/nvidia/cuda/tags`. A table of CUDA versions and GPU driver versions compatible with each CUDA version can be found at `https://github.com/NVIDIA/nvidia-docker/wiki/CUDA`.

In the preceding command, we specified that we wanted to use the NVIDIA Docker runtime using the `--runtime=nvidia` option. We can also run the same command without specifying the runtime by using the alias `nvidia-docker`, as follows:

```
$ nvidia-docker run --rm nvidia/cuda:9.0-base nvidia-smi
```

Running Caffe2 containers

The Caffe2 project provides Docker images for different versions of Caffe2 and Ubuntu, both for CPU and GPU. The full list of available Docker images can be found at `https://hub.docker.com/r/caffe2ai/caffe2/tags`. The Caffe2 image Docker tag describes its capabilities succinctly. For example, the `c2v0.8.1.cpu.min.ubuntu16.04` tag indicates that the image has Caffe2 v0.8.1 for CPU on Ubuntu 16.04.

The `c2v0.8.1.cuda8.cudnn7.ubuntu16.04` tag indicates that the image has Caffe2 v0.8.1 for GPU on Ubuntu 16.04 with CUDA 8.1 and cuDNN 7 installed.

We can spin up a Caffe2 CPU image and check whether Caffe2 works inside it in the following way:

```
$ docker run --rm -ti caffe2ai/caffe2:c2v0.8.1.cpu.min.ubuntu16.04
root@13588569ad8f:/# python -c "from caffe2.python import core"
WARNING:root:This caffe2 python run does not have GPU support. Will run in
CPU only mode.
```

We can spin up a Caffe2 GPU image and check whether Caffe2 works inside it in the following way:

```
$ nvidia-docker run --rm -ti
caffe2ai/caffe2:c2v0.8.1.cuda8.cudnn7.ubuntu16.04
root@9dd026974563:/# python -c "from caffe2.python import core"
```

Note how we need to use `nvidia-docker` instead of `docker` if we are using a Caffe2 GPU image.

Once your Caffe2 containers are working, you can mount your Caffe2 applications and data inside it and execute them. You can mount your host directories inside a Docker container using the `-v` option and indicating the guest directory to mount them to, as shown in the following example:

```
$ docker run --rm -ti -v /home/joe/caffe2_apps:/joe_caffe2_apps
caffe2ai/caffe2:c2v0.8.1.cpu.min.ubuntu16.04
```

This mounts your `/home/joe/caffe2_apps` directory as `/joe_caffe2_apps` inside the container. You are now ready to build Caffe2 applications inside containers and deploy those applications to servers locally or in the cloud using containers.

Caffe2 model visualization

DL models contain a high number of layers. Layers have many parameters, such as their name, type, weight dimensions, layer-type-specific parameters, input, and output tensor names. While typical feedforward network structures do not have cycles, the **Recurrent Neural Network** (**RNN**) and other network structures have cycles and other topologies. So, the ability to visualize the structure of a DL model is important, both for researchers devising new networks to solve problems, and for practitioners using new networks.

Visualization using Caffe2 net_drawer

Caffe2 ships with a simple visualization tool written in Python named net_drawer. This Python script can be found in your Caffe2 installation directory. For example, if you installed Caffe2 at /usr/local, then this tool is available at /usr/local/lib/python2.7/dist-packages/caffe2/python/net_drawer.py on your system. You can also find this tool in your Caffe2 source code at caff2/python/net_drawer.py.

We can visualize the AlexNet model from Chapter 4, *Working with Caffe*, using net_drawer, as follows:

```
$ python net_drawer.py --input /path/to/bvlc_alexnet/predict_net.pb --
rankdir TB
```

We are indicating that we want to visualize the nodes of the graph in a top-to-bottom order using the option --rankdir TB. This command renders the AlexNet graph shown in *Figure 4.3* in Chapter 4, *Working with Caffe*.

This command writes two files. The first is a text file named AlexNet.dot that holds the graph structure in the human-readable GraphViz DOT format. The second is a PDF file named AlexNet.pdf with a graphical rendering of the structure.

Note that this tool provides other options to customize the visualization. You can find these by using the --help option, as follows:

```
$ python net_drawer.py --help
usage: net_drawer.py [-h] --input INPUT [--output_prefix OUTPUT_PREFIX]
                     [--minimal] [--minimal_dependency] [--
                     append_output]
                     [--rankdir RANKDIR]

Caffe2 net drawer.
```

```
optional arguments:
  -h, --help              show this help message and exit
  --input INPUT           The input protobuf file.
  --output_prefix OUTPUT_PREFIX
                          The prefix to be added to the output filename.
  --minimal               If set, produce a minimal visualization.
  --minimal_dependency    If set, only draw minimal dependency.
  --append_output         If set, append the output blobs to the operator
                          names.
  --rankdir RANKDIR       The rank direction of the pydot graph.
```

Visualization using Netron

Netron is a browser based DL model visualization written in Python. It is open source and available at `https://github.com/lutzroeder/netron`.

Compared to `net_drawer`, Netron has a modern visualization style and allows a far better interaction with the graph nodes to view their parameters. Also, Netron's zoom capability makes it easier to use on larger networks. The biggest advantage of using Netron is that it supports the visualization of models from a large number of DL frameworks, such as Caffe2, Caffe, TensorFlow, and also the ONNX format.

Netron can be installed from PyPI repository using the following command:

```
$ pip3 install --user netron
```

We can visualize our Caffe2 AlexNet protobuf file using Netron, as follows:

```
$ netron -b /path/to/predict_net.pb
```

This opens a new tab in your browser at `http://localhost:8080` with a visualization of the AlexNet model. We can zoom in and out using the scroll feature of the mouse. Clicking on any layer in the model shows its parameters on the right. This can be seen in *Figure 7.2* for our AlexNet model, as follows:

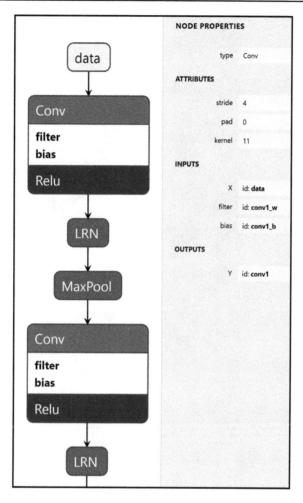

Figure 7.2: Netron visualization of AlexNet with the parameters of the first Convolution layer shown on the right

Summary

In the final chapter of this guide, we looked at two applications of Caffe2 that demonstrate its ability. As an application of Caffe2 to edge devices, we looked at how to build Caffe2 on the Raspberry Pi single-board computers and run Caffe2 applications on them. As an application of Caffe2 to the cloud, we looked at how to build and run Caffe2 applications inside Docker containers. As an aid to understanding the structure of DL models, we examined two tools that helped in the visualization of Caffe2 models.

Other Books You May Enjoy

If you enjoyed this book, you may be interested in these other books by Packt:

Deep Learning with PyTorch Quick Start Guide
David Julian

ISBN: 9781789534092

- Set up the deep learning environment using the PyTorch library
- Learn to build a deep learning model for image classification
- Use a convolutional neural network for transfer learning
- Understand to use PyTorch for natural language processing
- Use a recurrent neural network to classify text
- Understand how to optimize PyTorch in multiprocessor and distributed environments
- Train, optimize, and deploy your neural networks for maximum accuracy and performance
- Learn to deploy production-ready models

Deep Learning Quick Reference
Mike Bernico

ISBN: 9781788837996

- Solve regression and classification challenges with TensorFlow and Keras
- Learn to use Tensor Board for monitoring neural networks and its training
- Optimize hyperparameters and safe choices/best practices
- Build CNN's, RNN's, and LSTM's and using word embedding from scratch
- Build and train seq2seq models for machine translation and chat applications.
- Understanding Deep Q networks and how to use one to solve an autonomous agent problem.
- Explore Deep Q Network and address autonomous agent challenges.

Leave a review - let other readers know what you think

Please share your thoughts on this book with others by leaving a review on the site that you bought it from. If you purchased the book from Amazon, please leave us an honest review on this book's Amazon page. This is vital so that other potential readers can see and use your unbiased opinion to make purchasing decisions, we can understand what our customers think about our products, and our authors can see your feedback on the title that they have worked with Packt to create. It will only take a few minutes of your time, but is valuable to other potential customers, our authors, and Packt. Thank you!

Index

Protocol Buffers (ProtoBuf) 62
prototxt file 7, 62, 63, 64
PyTorch 8

R

Raspberry Pi
  about 104, 105
  Caffe2, used 103
Raspbian
  Caffe2, building on 106, 107, 108
  installing 105, 106
Rectified Linear Unit (ReLU) 35
Recurrent Neural Network (RNN) 113
ReLU layer
  composing 34, 35, 36
Relu operator, characteristics
  implementation 76
  name 76
  version 76
run 30

S

Sigmoid function 27
Sigmoid operator 27
Softmax function 29
Softmax operator 29
Stochastic Gradient Descent (SGD) 42, 53
Stretch 105
stride 45
support vector machines (SVM) 7

T

TensorRT installers

URL, for downloading 88
TensorRT
  API 93, 94
  execution context of engine, used for inference 92
  installing 88, 89, 90
  network, creating 90
  optimized engine, building from network 91
  pre-trained network, importing 90
  usage 93, 94
  using 90
training data 7
training layers, LeNet
  about 52
  accuracy layer 53, 54
  loss layer 52
  optimization layers 53

U

Ubuntu 9

V

validation data 56

W

weights 40

Y

Yangqing Jia 58

Z

zero padding 45

www.ingramcontent.com/pod-product-compliance
Lightning Source LLC
Chambersburg PA
CBHW080537060326
40690CB00022B/5152